Popular Orchids

Dendrobium nobile

POPULAR ORCHIDS

Brian and Wilma Rittershausen

DAVID & CHARLES : NEWTON ABBOT

ISBN 0 7153 4973 2

Set in 11/12 pt Times
and printed in Great Britain
by Bristol Typesetting Co Ltd
for David & Charles (Publishers) Limited
South Devon House Newton Abbot Devon

Contents

Illustrations

Plates

In Text

All drawings of plants and flowers are approximately one-quarter
below actual size

Drawings by Wilma Rittershausen

We gratefully acknowledge the kind assistance of Julia Brooks in producing most of the photographs for this book.

One

An Introduction To Orchids

Today the orchid is a plant far better understood than it has been at any time in the past. Gone are the old fallacies that tropical orchids coming from far-off lands can only be grown in a greenhouse with great heat and special skills. Gone also is the belief that orchids are only within the reach of the wealthy. Many years ago, when importation was a difficult and uncertain business, with man-made hybrids a rarity, this was certainly true. But today it is very much the reverse.

Anyone with a general interest in flowers cannot fail to see that the orchid stands apart from all other plant forms. The orchid belongs to one of the largest and most remarkable families of flowering plants in the world, which is also among the most beautiful. No one knows exactly how many natural species occur in the wild, and estimates vary from fifteen to thirty thousand. Whichever figure is taken it is most impressive, and to this can be added a further fifty thousand or so hybrids produced to date in orchid nurseries.

All orchids conform to a definite pattern, and yet every species is different. There appears to be no end to nature's imagination here. Orchids differ from other plants especially in the structure of their flowers. Where most flowers contain separate male and female organs, the stigma and stamens, orchids have a single central structure known as the column which contains both the male and female parts. At the end of this column is to be found the pollen in solid masses, known as pollinia, which can be two, four or occasionally eight in number. They are covered by a protective cap, the anther. Surrounding this central structure are three outer sepals and three petals. The two lateral petals usually have the same colouring and shape as the sepals, while the third petal is always different in some way from the rest of the flower: it is known as the lip or labellum. The lip is sometimes smaller than the petals but more often greatly exaggerated in size, brightly coloured and of a different shape to the rest of the flower. Its purpose is to form a platform upon which the visiting insect may alight before performing the act of fertilisation.

Here the orchid is truly remarkable in its efforts to ensure cross-pollination of its flowers. Some orchids depend upon mimicry for this deception, and for a brilliant example of this one need look no further than to our own native bee orchid, *Ophrys apifera*, the lip of which mimics a female bee.

All species of Ophrys carry out this deception: the orchids normally begin to flower when the male pollinating insects— which include bees and various kinds of fly—emerge, but before the female insects make their appearance, usually about three weeks later. During this time, the bee searching for a mate sees the orchid flower and alights on the lip. The orchid is designed not only to look like a female insect, but to smell and feel like one. By the time the male insect discovers his mistake—if indeed he does—the pollen masses are firmly attached to his head; he then flies to another flower where the pollinia are deposited on the stigma.

Other orchids rely upon a strong fragrance to attract a particular insect; this may be the sweet smell of nectar to attract bee or moth, or the odour of rotting meat which will bring forth carrion fly or wasp. For the same reason some orchids produce their fragrance at evening or early in the morning, depending upon the insect they wish to attract. In the comet orchid, *Angraecum sesquipedale*, we have a striking example of this. The orchid carries a long spur about one foot long, and it was predicted by Darwin that a moth with a proboscis of the same length must visit this flower to pollinate it. It was a considerable time later that this moth was discovered and Darwin's statement proved true.

A few orchids have a highly sensitive hinged lip, such as *Masdevallia muscosa*, which will snap shut when agitated by an insect. Another extreme is seen in the bucket orchid, *Coryanthes*, whose lip is formed into an appendage best described as a bucket, held underneath the flower. As the flower opens, it secretes an insect-attracting liquid to fill the bucket, into which the unfortunate insect falls. It is only by swimming to a 'funnel' at one end of the 'bucket' that it can escape, in doing which it presses against the column and thus removes the pollen.

The diversity and colour to be found among orchid flowers is endless, with every possible shade represented, including black. Some of these blooms are so small as to need the assistance of a magnifying glass to study their flora in any detail, while others may be as large as eight inches across. In one species of *Phragmipedium* the long ribbon-like petals reach downwards to a length of over two feet; when spreading these petals out sideways, it must surely be the largest flower in the world! Some flowers will last in perfection for up to three months, while a flowering head of *Epidendrum radicans* can be expected to produce a succession of flowers lasting for two years or more on a mature plant. Others produce exotic paper-thin blooms whose short life will be just two days.

In their habit of growth orchids can be just as surprising and remarkable as are their flowers. The plants can be small enough to be comfortably contained in a thimble, or twice the height of a man.

Many species produce pseudo-bulbs, which are swollen stems used for storage of water, joined by a creeping rhizome; a new bulb is added each growing season. These are known as Sympodials. Some varieties which do without pseudo-bulbs have a vertical rhizome with the leaves growing from the apex; these are known as Monopodials.

Orchids can be found on every continent of the world with the exception only of the arctic regions. But it is to the tropical countries that we must look for the most exotic and beautiful blooms. In their natural environment the most popular of the orchids under cultivation can be divided generally into two types.

The *epiphytes* grow upon the branches and trunks of trees, where they adhere to the bark with their thick roots which obtain all the nourishment required from the moisture rising from the jungle floor. The plant may also derive a weak form of fertiliser from bird droppings washed down the tree during heavy rain, and from debris collecting in the angles of the tree branches, into which the roots will penetrate. It is therefore a mistake to assume that because an orchid grows upon a tree it is a parasite, like the mistletoe. The orchid takes nothing from its host and simply enjoys the advantages afforded in the way of extra light, and extra room for growth and expansion. This way of life has been successfully adopted by the greater number of tropical orchids, but it is, of course, unpractical in cooler regions where exposed roots would suffer from the cold.

The *terrestrial* type of orchid, to which the bee orchid and all others found in Britain belong, grows from the ground, some of them managing with very little foliage, the main growth being a flower stalk where the foliage has evolved to small leafy bracts. One Australian species is known to exist entirely under the ground, with just the tips of the flowers protruding above the surface. But such orchids are exceptions, and only mentioned to show the extremes to which orchids will go; since this book is concerned with the popular varieties, they are only mentioned in passing.

The credit for first importing tropical orchids into Britain must be given to the early Victorians; Britain was the greatest importer of orchids in those days, and now probably leads the world in orchid knowledge and culture.

In those early days tropical orchids were imported in their

ten of thousands. As a result of long sea journeys and lack of knowledge many of them died. But by persevering the growers continued to improve their greenhouses and heating systems, and their knowledge of the orchids steadily grew. Soon orchid growing became an extremely popular hobby among the wealthy, and no town or country estate was complete without its prized collection of orchids.

The early hybridists encountered many difficulties in the raising of the seedlings until the 1920s. In this era the greatest step forward in seed raising was taken by the discovery of a method by which orchids could be raised artificially under sterile conditions, as opposed to sowing seed on soil. As a result many more hybrids were successfully raised, swelling the ranks to give us the vast selection available today. But although there are many thousands of species, only a very small minority of these have been used for hybridising, and today the species are quite as popular among amateurs as the latest modern hybrid.

In more recent years we have seen the introduction of a method of mass propagating an individual plant known as meristem culture (see Chapter 6, page 85), which must be regarded as another great milestone in the history of orchids. By this method a further market has been produced, giving the amateur the choice of the most modern hybrids at most reasonable prices, where previously a very high price was demanded for what might be the only plant of its kind.

Since the war there has been the most dramatic increase in amateur orchid growers, which confirms that orchids are easy plants that everyone who owns a greenhouse can grow. This has led to the formation of many orchid societies all over the country whose aims are to give genuine encouragement and advice to the beginner, and to enable the amateur to share his interest with fellow enthusiasts. Exhibitions organised by these societies do a great deal to further the growing interest in orchids.

The grower has at his disposal a wider range of orchids than ever before. Indeed, this range is perhaps greater than in any other flower, and the hybrids of tomorrow have the promise of being ever more beautiful.

Page 17: (*left*) *Odontoglossum grande*; (*above*) *Anguloa uniflora*

Page 18 : *Odontoglossum* Red Queen 'Burnham' AM

Two

General Culture

The successful growing of orchids in a greenhouse is the combination of several factors, each of which will be dealt with in detail. These factors are not placed in order of preference, as each is equally important to the welfare of the plants. If it were possible all would have been placed first on the list! It is, for example, of little use to maintain the correct temperatures while at the same time allowing the plants to suffer from insufficient water, and so on. Of all the cultural factors to be considered, we have discussed the temperatures first for several reasons. The maintenance of the required temperature is perhaps the most expensive item. Should the plants be subjected to one night without heat when the temperature in the greenhouse falls below freezing, this will undoubtedly kill them. But, should the grower fail to water or damp down his or her plants for several days, no permanent damage will result, and any harm can be quickly rectified.

Orchids can be grown in three basic temperature ranges known as cool, intermediate and hot. Which range we grow them in is determined by the prevailing conditions in the part of the world where they are found naturally. Hence it will be understood that the grower cannot expect to succeed with both strictly cool- and intermediate-house orchids unless separate greenhouses are available for them, or at least separate sections within a greenhouse. However, there are exceptions to this rule of nature, and a few intermediate orchids may be grown at the warmest end of a cool greenhouse, while some cool-growing orchids can be encouraged to do better in the intermediate house. Orchids such as Dendrobiums will do well when grown in the intermediate house during the summer and rested in the cool house for the winter.

THE COOL HOUSE

Temperatures. Many orchids in their natural environment flourish in mountainous regions, sometimes near the equator, often 8,000 ft above sea level. Although they can be subjected to violent extremes of temperature from very hot sunny days to freezing cold at night, owing to the rarity of the atmosphere at this elevation, the plants thrive. In the greenhouse all other conditions may be imitated to suit the orchids, except this rarity of the atmosphere which cannot be reproduced. It is for this reason that we keep orchids from these regions in a cool greenhouse where they are grown slightly warmer than the average temperature in nature. This also enables us to grow orchids from completely different parts of the world in harmony under the same greenhouse roof.

It does not follow that all the orchids grown in our cool greenhouses come from high altitudes. Many of them grow in naturally cool regions of the earth.

The artificial heating of a cool greenhouse will usually begin around the end of September and continue throughout the winter months until about the beginning of May. During the winter months the night temperature should be approximately 50°F (10°C) although on very severe cold nights an occasional drop to 45°F (7.2°C) will not affect the plants as long as they are kept on the dry side during these periods. It must be emphasised however, that plants cannot be kept at this temperature of 45° and be expected to grow. Therefore it is necessary to have a daytime temperature of at least 10° more, which may naturally rise higher on sunny days. The heating system should be adequate to maintain these temperatures easily in the coldest of winter spells.

During the summer months, when artificial heat is dispensed with, a natural night time temperature of at least 50° (10°C) can be maintained. These cool nights are essential for certain genera of orchids to produce their flowers. The daytime temperatures will be much higher and on hot sunny days may rise as high as 75° to 80° F (23.9° to 26.7°C) but should not be allowed to go higher. Should the temperature soar into the hundreds then the greenhouse is not correctly ventilated and shaded, and these extremes can be as detrimental to the plants as too low a temperature on a winter's night. The following chart may be taken as a guide, bearing in mind the points mentioned above.

	WINTER	SUMMER
DAY	60°F to 65°F 16°C to 18°C	60°F to 80F° 16°C to 27°C
NIGHT	48°F to 50°F 9°C to 10°C	50°F to 52°F 10°C to 11°C

Humidity. The humidity must at all times be in a correct balance with the temperature—high in high temperatures, low in cold conditions. The atmospheric moisture in the greenhouse is created by damping down, a routine job usually carried out in the morning when the temperature is rising. The paths and floor beneath the staging and the staging itself are soaked with water which can be used straight from the mains; thus conserving the rain water for the actual watering of the plants. All surfaces should be thoroughly wetted, not forgetting the back of the staging and areas out of sight. During the summer when the light intensity is high and the plants are growing fast, they will benefit from as much atmospheric moisture as can be given them. On bright sunny days the plants will enjoy an overhead spray several times during the day, but making sure the foliage is dry by nightfall.

There are times, both during summer and winter, when we experience dull, sunless days, when there is sufficient

moisture in the atmosphere to make damping down unnecessary for a day or two. On the other hand during severe
wintry weather when bright sunny days are followed by
severe frosty nights, the temperature may fluctuate greatly and
the amount of artificial heat necessary will cause much drying out of the house, so that extra attention to damping down
will be necessary, particularly in areas close to the heating
system. At this time humidity trays should be kept full of
water and gravelled staging should be well damped.

Damping down during the winter should always be done on
a rising temperature and not after midday, thus ensuring that
all surplus moisture will have evaporated before nightfall.
During very cold spells of wintry weather, when there may be
difficulty in maintaining the correct temperature, the humidity
must remain low, otherwise this will cause the spotting of
flowers, and over a period cause black marks and other diseases
of the foliage. Where these conditions prevail virus disease in
particular will be encouraged.

Ventilation. Fresh air is something all orchids enjoy and should
be provided whenever conditions permit. In the early part of
the year the ventilators should be opened in the morning,
after the damping down has been done, a little at a time as the
temperature rises. Depending upon the prevailing weather,
they may be left open until the afternoon. An electric fan will
circulate the air, keeping the greenhouse fresh and buoyant,
and avoiding any stagnation of the atmosphere.

During July and August it is possible to leave the ventilators
fully open all day from early morning, with a 'crack' of air
at night. Remembering that this will reduce the moisture in the
greenhouse, it should be well damped down during this period.
Towards the end of the summer the ventilators should be closed
down at night, and as the autumn advances they should be
closed earlier in the day, thus conserving as much of the natural
heat as possible, at a time when artificial heating has not yet
commenced.

The opportunities of opening the ventilators during the winter are often few, and it may only be possible to give fresh air for a short while on the opposite side of the greenhouse to the prevailing wind. The vents should be opened just a crack to give gentle ventilation, avoiding a cold draught which will cause a sudden drop in temperature. It is important that during the winter, ventilation is only applied where the temperature is well above the minimum required; half an hour will be sufficient to freshen up the air inside the greenhouse. At this time of the year the electric fan comes into its own, and can be left on day and night, there being no loss of valuable heat as would occur with ventilation.

Where a greenhouse is built with bottom ventilation below staging level, these vents may be used with advantage during the summer in conjunction with the top ventilators to cause a gentle upward movement of air through the greenhouse. In the winter they can be used when one is unable to open the top ventilators without causing a draught. Although not many greenhouses are built with bottom vents today, they are nevertheless useful for orchids, and better than side ventilators at staging level, which are too close to the plants and will dry them out too quickly.

Shading. During the summer months the shading of the greenhouse is the main factor in keeping the inside temperature down, when the house has been thoroughly damped and fully ventilated. Where an amateur finds that the temperature in his or her small greenhouse gets uncomfortably high on sunny days, a thick coat of white greenhouse shading will reflect the heat and keep the temperature down. The shading is thick enough if one can look at the sun through the glass without it hurting the eyes. This paint shading may be used on its own, or in conjunction with wooden lath blinds, in which case a thinner coat of shading would be put on. Where lath blinds are used, these should be on the outside of the house, with a gap of about nine inches between them and the glass, where they will not only shade the glass but help to keep it cool. Inside blinds made of dark polythene are not suitable, for they tend to attract the heat, making the house hotter instead of cooler.

By the end of August into early September, the shading should be gradually reduced. The paint shading is usually thinned down sufficiently by the weather, otherwise it can be washed off.

During the winter the orchids will enjoy full light as the days are short and there is little power in the sun. From February onwards one must be aware of the bright sunny days. Even though the weather may still be cold, this early spring sunshine can be harmful to young growths and flowers. A thin coat of shading should be applied, which may be washed off again quite quickly by heavy rain or late snow, and it will therefore be necessary to thicken it up as the year advances. Should an emergency arise where one has hot sun burning down upon the plants at such a time, before any shading has been put on, it may be a good idea to place sheets of newspaper gently over the plants to provide sufficient shade until such time as one is able to get the job of shading properly done. During heavy rain, when the shading is washed off, steps must be taken to prevent the dirty water from entering the water tank.

The ideal form of shading is undoubtedly lath blinds which can be rolled up and down to suit the immediate weather conditions. During the spring months when we experience bright bursts of sunshine they will be brought into use, perhaps only two or three times in a week. If in doubt better to leave down. Even during the summer on dull cloudy days the blinds may remain rolled up. Blinds can also be installed to work automatically, operated by an electric motor which is controlled by the prevailing weather.

Watering. The orchids with which we are concerned in this book are neither bog nor desert plants, and cannot stand such extremes. However, at certain times of the year the plants are resting and will need little or no water; and during their growing season, when they have plenty of active, fast-developing roots, they may absorb copious supplies of water to enable them to make up large, healthy pseudo-bulbs in the time available. It is essential always to avoid letting the compost get sodden; a well-drained material will allow air and water to filter freely through the pot, at the same time allowing sufficient moisture to be retained for the plant.

The orchids should be watered with a spouted can, using rainwater at greenhouse temperature. Always water from the rim of the pot until the whole surface is thoroughly flooded to overflowing. This should disappear within a few seconds when the surface may be flooded again if necessary. Water that lies on the surface of the compost forming a lingering puddle is usually an indication either that the plant was far too dry and had been previously underwatered, or that the compost is too firmly packed in the pot. On the other hand, should the water disappear too rapidly, this means the compost is too loose. It may be that the plant has not been repotted for a long time and most of the substance in the compost has decomposed. The principle of watering little and often, giving a dribble here and a dribble there is courting disaster. One good, thorough watering is the golden rule, giving no more until the plant requires it.

Orchids growing in baskets should be dipped in the water tank and left there for a few minutes until the compost stops bubbling. Plants attached to pieces of wood etc, with long aerial roots, should be kept moist by regular daily spraying. These aerial roots will also absorb a certain amount of moisture from the atmosphere in between sprays.

An orchid plant needs water when the compost has become dry, but before it has become completely bone-dry. This can be determined by feeling the compost, by lifting the pot to judge its weight, or by tapping the edge of the pot and listening to the resulting sound. Any of these methods will give an indication as to whether a plant is wet or dry. Where the sphagnum moss is growing freely upon a surface, this can be used as a very good guide. While the moss remains a green colour, the plant is sufficiently wet. As the compost begins to dry out the moss will turn from green to grey. This is the time to water, when the moss will soon resume its green colour. If the plant is allowed to remain dry, the moss will turn from grey to white and eventually die—unsatisfactory for both the moss and the plant! Where an economy compost is used, it can readily be seen when the peat is dry.

Watering should always be carried out in the morning when the temperature is rising, and preferably on a sunny morning. This is most important during the winter, to ensure that all surface water has evaporated by dusk. If in doubt it is better to leave a particular plant until the following day.

There is no hard and fast rule on frequency of watering, but the collection should be inspected at least every other day and those individual plants that need it should then be watered. It may be that a small plant is watered twice or three times in a week during the summer, while a much larger plant will remain wet for up to ten days. Much depends upon the time of year as well as the immediate weather conditions.

Under-watering a plant is the most common fault met in an amateur's greenhouse. For fear of over-watering, a plant is often well-meaningly left dry for too long a period, the result being shrivelled pseudo-bulbs and limp foliage. Compost and pot become so thoroughly dry that one application of water is swiftly absorbed by the clay-pot before the roots have a chance to take it up. This is a case where the plant should be submerged in a bucket to just above the rim of the pot and allowed to soak.

A growing plant should never be allowed to become so dry that when dropped into the bucket is actually floats. When an orchid has become this dry, the roots and bulbs will shrivel and growth will be slowed down until the plant is at rest; and an enforced rest during the growing season is bad for the

plant and will lead to retarded growth. To get the plant growing again, usually the first job will be to repot it into fresh
compost. Once the compost has become very dry over a long
period it will be difficult to wet again, and in any case much
of its food value will have been lost. After repotting, regular
spraying of the foliage will prevent moisture loss through the
leaves until new roots get under way. With correct watering
from now on the new roots will be encouraged to grow, and
after several weeks, or maybe months, the plant will gradually plump up and continue its growing cycle.

If a plant has been overwatered, the rule of allowing it to
dry out between each watering has not been observed. It may
be that the plant has been standing directly under a drip
from the greenhouse roof. In either case, a completely sodden
compost will lead to a prematurely decomposed and 'sour' condition. The plant will outwardly resemble the underwatered
plant with shrivelled pseudo-bulbs or limp foliage; this has
resulted from the loss of roots through drowning or suffocating.

The overwatered plant must be removed from its pot immediately, and the blackened rotten roots removed. If much
of the foliage has been lost it will be necessary to reduce the
size of the plant. In the case of a Cymbidium, for example,
that has lost all foliage except for the leading pseudo-bulb,
it should be reduced to just two or three bulbs, and these be
repotted into as small a pot as possible in pure fresh sphagnum
moss. Very careful watering will be required, and overhead
spraying until new active roots appear and the plant starts
the long journey back to health.

Resting. Epiphytes growing in the wild are subjected to daily
downpours of heavy rain, while at other times of the year
they have to contend with long periods of drought. During
this latter period, in nature, the plant ceases all growth and a
percentage of the foliage is shed as the roots stop. The
whole plant is now dormant and at rest, and the pseudo-bulbs
are ripened prior to their flowering. It is the large reserves of

energy stored up in these pseudo-bulbs that the plants rely on to produce their flowers during this time. In many species this occurs before the plant has started its new growth. The terrestrial orchids with which we are concerned here are growing in a more constant moisture state throughout the year and therefore require little or no resting at all.

The British winter corresponds with this natural resting period of the orchids. Therefore in the autumn, when growth is completed and the pseudo-bulbs are plump and firm, they are ready to begin their rest. Many of the species are now moved to the coolest end of the greenhouse where they are placed on shelves as close to the glass as possible to give the maximum light, which is essential to ensure complete ripening of their bulbs. At the same time watering is gradually reduced and in some plants dispensed with altogether. While in this inactive state the natural process of shrivelling will take place in some species. This slight shrivelling of the pseudo-bulbs is quite in order and is essential if the plants are to flower properly. It is not to be confused with the dangerous shrivelling caused through incorrect watering as previously discussed.

With the Vandas and their allies the very thick aerial roots will cease to grow at the tips, and a white papery covering will encase them, a sure indication that the plant is resting.

Except for young seedlings which should be grown continuously without any checks to their growth, most orchids will need some form of rest. This may differ from a few weeks to several months. Only inactive plants should be rested. It does sometimes happen that a particular plant which is about to be rested produces new growth instead. In this case the new growth must take precedence and the plant be kept growing.

There is no doubt that certain orchids are more free-flowering than others and again, if we look to their wild state, it will be seen that some plants reproduce themselves quite adequately by vegetative means, and therefore do not need to be so free-flowering; the future of the species is ensured by their continually dividing and sub-dividing. On the other hand others —by the very nature of their precarious habitat such as growing on dead trees—must reproduce themselves by the more positive method of flowering and seeding, if their species is to continue to exist.

It will often be found that a few plants in a collection have proved themselves over a number of years to be shy flowering. With such plants a more severe winter rest is called for. This is often all that is wrong with an otherwise healthy plant which is growing well and producing good-sized pseudo-bulbs which one would expect to flower.

With the approach of spring, the new growths will appear. This is a sign that the plant is waking up and once again on the move. At this time the plants should be repotted into fresh compost, and returned to their summer quarters. The new growth is usually preceded by the development of new roots, and it is when the new roots appear that watering can gradually be recommenced. Apply water perhaps once a week to begin with and more frequently as the growth and roots advance, taking care not to allow water into the new growth. Any shrivelled pseudo-bulbs will quickly plump up as the roots penetrate the new compost. From this time on normal culture can be resumed.

Feeding. Orchids can be grown with complete success without the aid of any artificial feeding. Because they are slow-growing plants they cannot consume great quantities of nourishment at a time, and will find sufficient for their needs in the compost provided. The beginner would be wise not to attempt the feeding of his or her orchids, apart from the recommended sprinkle of bone meal added when repotting. Artificial feeding can be harmful to orchids, and through overfeeding a plant can become too lush and of too soft a growth to be capable of producing flowers. It will also encourage a type of virus in the form of black flecking to appear on some orchids.

While we state that feeding is not necessary, and can be harmful when carried out by an inexperienced grower, we would also mention that a carefully planned feeding programme, properly and intelligently carried out by a grower who thoroughly understands his orchids, can be of benefit, encouraging the plants to do that little bit better, and producing ever bigger and better flowers more frequently.

First it must be understood which orchids to feed, and which not to feed. Generally speaking, the terrestrials will appreciate feeding rather than the epiphytes.

A plant can only be fed during its growing season, when it is growing strongly, and is producing plenty of active roots. Orchids should never be fed during the winter months. The plants are neither growing fast enough, nor is the light intensity sufficient in this country. At the beginning of the season one may commence with a weak fertiliser solution, say once in every four waterings. This is gradually increased to mid-summer when the maximum feed is given, to be reduced again as the autumn approaches. This steady, even feeding should always be of the same brand or made-up solution. There is a danger of overstepping the recommended dose, and as has been seen this can lead to trouble.

Where a feeding programme is being undertaken, one's culture must be adjusted accordingly. Extra light will be needed by the plants to balance the extra amount of food, bearing in mind that they will be growing faster.

There are many proprietary brands of fertiliser, both organic and inorganic, which are ideal for greenhouse plants and which may be used quite safely on orchids when mixed to the manufacturers' recommended strength. These fertilisers give the best control over a feeding programme: one knows exactly what chemicals one's plants are receiving, and in what proportions. In this way it is possible to avoid a build-up of salts in the compost. Several of the fertilisers can be used as a foliar feed, applied with a rosed can or syringe.

Alternatively, one can make one's own feed from a butt in

the garden filled with water containing bone meal or cow manure. When this has become well fermented, it can be administered to the plants well diluted to have the appearance of weak tea.

Ailments. The most common ailments in orchids are black tips and patches occurring on the foliage. Apart from the diseases discussed in Chapter Five these can be caused by such bad cultural methods as overwatering, previously mentioned, cold draughts, or a combination of any of these. During the summer ugly black patches can be the result of sun-scorch.

These signs are a warning; and the remedy is to adjust one's culture accordingly. Black tips may be trimmed back for appearance's sake. Yellow leaves that appear on the older bulbs during the autumn or immediately after repotting are quite natural and nothing to worry about. However, should excessive loss of foliage occur at any time there may be some cause for concern. It may be the plant has become sickly for some reason, and this can be determined by knocking the plant out of its pot and examining the roots. From the condition of these it will be possible to tell whether the plant has been overwatered, or the roots attacked by some pest such as a slug. Alternatively, the compost may be found to be in a very poor state which has resulted in the loss of roots. The remedy is to repot into sphagnum moss, having first reduced the number of pseudo-bulbs accordingly.

Soft pseudo-bulbs sometimes occur for no apparent reason, possibly the result of damage. They should be removed to prevent the rot spreading, by cutting down to the rhizome and carefully dusting the severed area with powdered sulphur or charcoal. Upon examination of the severed pseudo-bulb, it may be possible to determine the cause of the rot.

New growths which suddenly become transparent to brown may have had water lodging inside them overnight. They should be cut back to the rhizome and the plant treated with sulphur or charcoal.

Any plant which has had a rotting part cut away should be placed on a shelf where it can be kept a little dryer until the wound has healed and completely dried up. In a very short while the plant should produce a further new growth.

A plant whose foliage has turned from a dark healthy green to a sickly yellow may be suffering from starvation; this is especially so with fast-growing seedlings in small pots. The important point here is to be able to recognise this condition and repot accordingly. An overhead spray with a foliar feed will help the foliage to regain its green colour.

Certain orchids, notably the *Phalaenopsis* and *Oncidium papilio* will sometimes over-flower themselves to the detriment of the plant. This they should not be allowed to do, and when the flowers are seen to become smaller and smaller, the spikes should be removed and the plant encouraged to grow.

In a healthy plant the pseudo-bulbs will get larger as the plant matures. If the reverse is the case and a plant produces a smaller pseudo-bulb each year, something is obviously wrong. One should take a long hard look at one's culture to see where improvement is necessary. In these instances, it will be a long time before such a plant can regain sufficient energy and size of pseudo-bulb capable of producing flowers. Also, where a plant has become weakened through bad culture, it is more vulnerable to pests and diseases.

The loss of buds just prior to their opening is a most disappointing climax to months of watching and waiting. The most usual cause of this is again cold or damp, or a combination of the two. Also severe overwatering or underwatering will have the same effect on the buds. The course of action is again to adjust one's culture.

Where paraffin heaters are used for heating, fumes from ill-adjusted burners could be a possible cause of bud drop. The foregoing also applies to flower stems that have wilted and turned brown.

THE INTERMEDIATE AND HOT HOUSE

For the grower who is fortunate enough to have three green-houses or one which is large enough to be divided into three sections to accommodate the three main temperature groups, his range is indeed unlimited. He can grow plants from every continent in the world, including both species and hybrids, and his collection will be enhanced with a display of blooms all the year round.

So far in this chapter we have looked at the conditions needed by orchids coming from the temperate regions. For those orchids which grow naturally in warmer climates and which are sub-tropical, an intermediate section is provided. For the tropical types, which originate from the hotter regions of the world, it is necessary to provide even more heat in the form of a hot house or, as it was once known, a 'stove house'.

Not only will the intermediate house require a higher temperature than the cool house, but it will mean that artificial heat will have to be used for a much longer period. It will be necessary to turn on the heating earlier in the autumn and carry it on for longer in the spring. Correspondingly, in the hot house it will be necessary to maintain this artificial heat for almost the complete year. After the hottest of summer days it will be found that the natural night-time temperature is too low for these plants, and a little gentle heat will be required.

The temperatures given in the following chart are essential for the intermediate and hot greenhouses.

| | INTERMEDIATE HOUSE | |
	WINTER	SUMMER
DAY	60°F to 65°C	70°F to 80°F
	16°C to 18°C	21°C to 27°C
NIGHT	55°F	60°F to 65°F
	13°C	16°C to 18°C

| | HOT HOUSE | |
	WINTER	SUMMER
DAY	70°F to 75°F	75°F to 85°F
	21°C to 24°C	24°C to 30°C
NIGHT	60°F to 65°F	60°F to 65°F
	16°C to 18°C	16°C to 18°C

It is very important with these higher temperatures there should be a correspondingly high humidity. Damping down will generally be required more frequently as the houses dry out quicker. Well-gravelled staging and humidity trays filled with water will play an essential part in maintaining this high humidity.

Ventilation must be applied with far more care and attention. What can be a refreshing breeze in the cool house could be a cold draught in the hot house, where the inhabitants are far more susceptible to chills and greater care must be taken to ensure the house is draught-proof.

It would be false economy to decrease the amount of shade in an effort to take advantage of the natural sunshine to keep up the required temperature. Many of these hotter-growing orchids are just as much shade-loving plants as their cooler-growing cousins. The shading will assist in maintaining a more even temperature, as rapid fluctuations are to be avoided.

During the summer months the plants will take considerable amounts of water, never being allowed to become completely dry. Feeding can be given in slightly stronger doses than to the cool-house orchids.

Some of the warmer-growing plants will need a resting period during the winter and throughout this time water is withheld until they commence their new growth. During severe spells of wintry weather, when difficulty is experienced in keep-

Page 35: (*above*) *Cymbidium* Larne (standard), *Cymbidium* Pumilow (miniature); (*below*) *Cymbidium* Goblin 'Burnham'

Page 36: (*left*)
Dendrobium spectabile
'Burnham' AM
(*below*)
Anoectochilus regalis

ing up the required temperature, the less water around the house the better, and the plants may be left on the dry side until warmer conditions prevail.

Three

The Orchid Greenhouse

The orchid greenhouse may consist of a single-span or double-span roof. It may be a modest lean-to or conservatory. Orchids are very adaptable plants and more or less any type of structure may be converted to accommodate them, provided that adequate light, temperature and humidity can be provided.

It is for this reason that it is difficult to grow orchids as house plants. While the light is usually poor and the temperature fluctuates far too much, the humidity will be too low. Thus the orchids that will survive in the home are limited to a few of the hardier types which may survive for a few years rather than thrive as they would in a greenhouse. However, if circumstances demand that the orchids are grown indoors, we would suggest that they be accommodated in a glass case where they may be stood on a tray of damp gravel, and the glass cover will afford to the plants their own atmosphere and environment. Again this is only suitable to certain of the smaller growing types but here one may expect to be more successful than when standing the plants on a window-sill in an open room.

As mentioned above any type of greenhouse may be suitable for orchids, but where a new house is to be erected to accommodate them the builder would be well advised to choose his site wisely. An open site in the garden is preferred, well away from any large overhanging trees, but at the same time taking advantage of any wall or hedge that may act as a natural break against the prevailing wind. If the structure is to be a conservatory, one should choose a southerly aspect, providing the maximum natural light and warmth from the winter sun. A northerly aspect can produce very dark and cold conditions during the same period, thus adding to the fuel bill. Ideally, the greenhouse should run from north to south so that the sun passes over it and the plants inside all obtain the full benefit of the light.

The floor of the greenhouse should be earth with a concrete or gravel path. The walls up to staging level should be made of brick or concrete blocks, and the sides and roof of the house may be framed in either timber or metal. There are various transparent plastic materials available for glazing, but for orchids glass is preferred.

The greenhouse should be built as long as possible, for which there are two sound reasons. Firstly, it is more difficult to control the temperature in a small greenhouse, both in summer and winter; during the summer small houses are liable to become extremely hot, while during the winter the opposite will occur. Again, it is difficult to maintain correct humidity during the summer since atmospheric moisture is quickly lost because the ventilators need to be wide open in an endeavour to keep the temperature down. The second reason is that, without doubt, the time will arise for the enthusiast when his collection of orchids has outgrown his house, and he will be faced with the problem of enlarging the greenhouse, for he will find it unthinkable to dispose of any of his collection. Therefore, no matter what size is built, one should always look ahead and leave room to lengthen the greenhouse in the future.

In this age of automation the orchid grower may take full advantage of the modern equipment available, which will do away with the drudgery of stoking the boiler last thing at night or worrying while away on holiday whether the vents should have been opened or closed before departure. These essential operations can be fully taken care of with automation.

Heating. The heating system should first of all be completely reliable, and whatever type is chosen it should be easily able to maintain the minimum temperature required at all times without overtaxing the system. It is less expensive in the long run to have several sources of heat around the greenhouse, each giving off a gentle warmth and distributing the heat evenly, rather than one unit working at maximum capacity to produce all the heat in one small area. For example, where hot water pipes are installed, they should never be too hot to touch and it would be better to have an extra row of piping. In any case, it is always a good idea to have ready a reserve system of heating, which may be brought into use in an emergency.

The heating system may consist of a boiler with 4 inch flow and return hot water pipes, which should be at least nine inches below the staging and have a good clearance of air around them. The boiler may be hand stoked with solid fuel, but gas or oil firing permits automatic thermostatic control. The essential point is that the chimney should be tall enough to carry all fumes or smoke clear away from the building.

One of the most popular methods of heating today is by electricity. This can be easy to install and maintain and at the same time is completely labour-free when controlled by a thermostat. This can be more efficient than a boiler as there is no unnecessary consumption of fuel on a sunny day when the temperature is high enough from the sun's warmth. The electric heating may be from tubular bars or fan heaters. Fan heaters with built-in thermostats are particularly good as they circulate the air around the greenhouse, thus keeping a very even temperature. Fan heaters should be stood on the floor and the flow of hot air not directed straight at any plants. It should be remembered that this form of heating will dry out the atmosphere quicker, necessitating more frequent damping down.

Blue flame paraffin heaters are a further method of heating which has been used successfully for many years. While these lamps are ideal for a small greenhouse there is always a danger of their burning up too much of the atmosphere or giving off slight fumes which, although undetectable, can have disastrous effects upon tender buds which are very susceptible to fumes, although the plants themselves may not be affected. For this reason it is very important to keep the wick perfectly clean and to attach an airpipe leading from the heater to the outside. These heaters are usually supplied with humidity trays which should be kept topped up with water. The paraffin lamp can also be a useful reserve heater, to be used in cases of severe weather conditions or a breakdown of the main system.

In some cases where there is a lean-to or conservatory, the central heating of the dwelling house may be successfully extended to heat the orchids.

Whichever form of heating is chosen it should be installed by an expert and maintained according to the manufacturer's instructions.

It is also essential to have in the greenhouse two minimum/maximum thermometers placed in different positions so that a check can be kept on the lowest temperature recorded during the night.

Conservation of heat. This can be just as important as the actual heating of the house. With an old greenhouse, all draughts such as holes, gaps in the glass or badly fitting doors and ventilators should be attended to. Double glazing is a great asset for keeping up the temperature, particularly on cold windy nights. This is usually included in the original construction of the house, where provision is made for an extra layer of glass to be fixed to the inside of the house. This glass is not usually a permanent fixture, but allowance is made for it to be easily removed for cleaning purposes, or the gradual build-up of dirt and condensation in the cavity will reduce the amount of light reaching the plants. Polythene sheeting, which is cheaper and lighter to install, may also be used to advantage. It can be used as a complete liner for the whole of the greenhouse, making a considerable difference by reducing draughts and increasing the temperature. Polythene soon becomes covered in condensation and must therefore be erected very carefully, avoiding any wrinkles or creases which will cause harmful drips. This is an inexpensive material but it quickly becomes discoloured and dirty, and it is advisable to renew it annually.

Where it is intended to divide the greenhouse into two or three sections providing accommodation for cool, intermediate and hot house orchids, polythene or glass may be used and to save valuable space a dividing door may be replaced with a polythene curtain.

Staging. The staging provided should be at a height which allows the proposed varieties of plants to be grown with sufficient headroom when in full flower. A single staging consisting of asbestos sheeting covered in gravel to retain the moisture is quite sufficient, with the plants standing on upturned pots. Alternatively, an extra staging of open slats may be erected a few inches above the gravelled asbestos; both methods will allow a free movement of air around the plants. A two-inch lip may be added along the edge of the upper staging to prevent any small pots being knocked off the front.

Even in the smallest of greenhouses, provision should be made for a simple propagating frame consisting of wooden sides with a glass top and possibly a soil-warming cable, which can be most useful for starting back-bulbs, propagating etc, also for very young seedlings or hospitalising the occasional sick plant.

Somewhere under the staging, well out of the way, provision should be made for a tank in which to store an adequate supply of water at greenhouse temperature. This can be connected by a pipe to the gutter outside the greenhouse for collecting rain water.

The greenhouse should have top ventilators on both sides of the ridge, so that they may always be opened on the leeward side to the prevailing wind. Here again automation may be brought into play by the use of a non-electric device which, controlled by the temperature inside the house, will open or close the ventilator at a preset temperature. Bottom or side ventilation is useful with certain genera of orchids, but not essential, although it may be very useful in extremely hot weather for keeping temperatures down.

Fans. One of the main problems with a small greenhouse is that in the winter valuable heat and humidity can be quickly lost through opening the ventilators, and it is a good idea to install a small, inexpensive electric fan at one end of the greenhouse, placed well above the plants under the ridgeboard. This can be most beneficial in keeping the air fresh and the plants cool. During the summer such a fan will assist, in conjunction with the ventilators, in keeping the orchids cool.

A movement of air is very beneficial to some types of orchids, and the fan can be left on permanently without doing any harm at all.

Sprinklers. Sprinklers can be most useful for the person away from his greenhouse all day. When geared to work automatically they will keep the house moist and fresh on sunny days. They may be installed under the staging for damping down, or above the plants for spraying the foliage.

Shading. When it comes to shading the greenhouse there are a number of alternative ways to choose from, depending upon the amount of light required for the types of orchids grown. The best but most expensive form of shading are roller blinds made of slatted wood which can be rolled up or down depending upon the weather. An alternative method, but just as effective, is a paint shading applied to the outside of the glass with a distemper brush or with a syringe. When mixed to the maker's instructions this shading will clean off quite easily in the autumn. It is usually available in green and white, but white is usually preferred as this will reflect more heat than a darker colour and keep the greenhouse cooler.

Four

Composts and Repotting

It will be understood from the introductory chapter that the majority of orchids under cultivation are epiphytes. Therefore an organic compost is necessary for their requirements. As most orchids are slow growing the compost most used consists of materials that are slow to decompose. For many years the accepted base of any compost has been fresh sphagnum moss and osmunda fibre.

As well as providing food for the plant, sphagnum moss is a good moisture retainer and keeps the acidity of the compost in correct balance. It can be beneficial to the plant by assisting the production of new roots and is always used for propagating back-bulbs and to assist the recovery of any sick plant which may have lost its roots. Sphagnum moss is always used green and freshly gathered. In this state it will, in a short time grow over the surface of the compost, where it is an invaluable aid to future watering of the plant. When correctly used, it is slow to decompose. Sphagnum moss is readily obtainable from orchid nurseries and may be found growing wild in many parts of the country in bogs and marshy places.

Osmunda fibre is the root of the osmunda fern and is available from orchid nurseries, who obtain it mostly from Japan and Italy. The cost involved unfortunately makes it rather an expensive commodity. Because of its long-lasting quality and hard wiry texture, osmunda fibre will, when mixed with sphagnum moss, keep the compost open and freely drained. As well

45

as providing nourishment and food, it allows a plant to remain undisturbed for several years. Osmunda fibre may be purchased in any quantity and if kept in a dry condition will last indefinitely. The sphagnum moss, being always used fresh, should be obtained in smaller quantities as needed. Therefore the moss and fibre are better obtained as separate materials to be mixed together when required.

Sphagnum moss is usually available in long strands with a certain amount of foreign mosses, sticks and grass included. The worst of this should be picked out and the moss cut into suitable lengths depending upon the size of the plants to be potted. For example, if plants are to be potted into 2 to 4in pots, the moss should be approximately 1 to 2in long; for 6in pots and over, lengths of 3 to 4in will be required.

Osmunda fibre can be purchased in large clumps or ready cut for pulling. The strands will need pulling apart and chopping like the moss. If at all dusty, the fibre should be lightly sieved, using a fine grade of sieve.

It now remains to mix these two prepared materials thoroughly together to the required proportions. The compost can be used as it is with the addition of a pinch of bone meal or hoof and horn meal near the base of the container. Alternatively, other ingredients may be added in small quantities to suit particular orchids: thus loam or peat can be included in the compost of Cymbidiums and Paphiopedilums. Most of the soil should be sieved out and only the fibrous material used. Oak and beech leaves are suitable for all orchids; the flaky material should be used dry and crisp and rubbed small. Bracken may be used to help out with the osmunda fibre with all orchids, used brown and crisp and chopped to requirements. Both the fronds and stalks can be used.

With the ever-increasing cost and scarcity of osmunda fibre, many orchid growers are now using an alternative economy compost consisting of two other basic materials, peat and sand. The peat may be any of the brands available, such as the fine Irish sphagnum peat, or even a coarse lumpy peat. It should be thoroughly soaked and allowed to drain a day or so before use. Coarse sand or grit should be added to keep the mixture open, using up to 50 per cent depending upon the grade of peat used. To this basic compost may be added a small amount of chopped bracken, to aerate the compost further. Plastic chips and fibres, or granulated polystyrene, may be used as alternatives to sand.

There are a number of non-resinous tree barks available which can be used on their own as a complete compost. Different sizes of bark chips are used according to the size of the plant. Where pure bark is used there is the advantage of easy potting. The bark is simply poured in around the plant while it is held in position. Until a plant has become established a little difficulty may be experienced in getting it to remain upright; this can be overcome with the use of a wire stake clipped on to the edge of the pot. Bark is a fairly solid and substantial material which will last for several years, although after the first year it may be necessary to assist with a little food, such as liquid cow manure, greatly diluted.

With the economy compost mentioned above, a plant is quickly repotted and little skill is required, but the compost does decompose quicker, often making annual repotting necessary. Also more skill is required with the watering can, owing to the nature of the peat; unless well drained it can become sodden, or at the other extreme, if much underwatered it is very difficult to wet again thoroughly. On the other hand, plants potted in sphagnum moss and osmunda fibre, while requiring more skill in repotting, will remain in the same pot for several years, and it is easier for the amateur to give them a more constant degree of moisture.

Whichever compost is preferred it should be adhered to. It will do a plant no good to be switched from one to another. Should it be necessary to change the compost to a different type, all existing compost should be removed from the plant so as to avoid a pot filled half with one type and half with another.

It will be seen from the foregoing that orchids will grow successfully in a wide variety of composts provided one's culture, in particular watering, is adapted to their varying consistencies. For this reason no hard and fast rules have been laid down as to the proportions of materials that should make up a compost. Where we have suggested a 50-50 mix, this need be only approximate. More important, although this is not always realised, is the subsequent treatment the plant will receive after repotting. If the grower knows he is heavyhanded with the watering can, he would be well advised, with a moss and fibre compost, to use a little more proportionately of the latter; while the person who tends to underwater his plants may find it beneficial to add a little extra sphagnum. When economy composts are being made up, again the proportions mentioned may not be strictly adhered to, and these may vary according to the materials available in the locality. Where, for example, Cornish grit is to replace sand, a slightly smaller quantity would be required. At the same time, the grade of peat used must be taken into consideration. The coarser the grade, the less sand will be required. With a little experience the grower will be able to judge simply from the look and feel of the compost whether it is of a good mix.

The spring is the best time to undertake any repotting, when the new growths are getting under way, and the new roots soon to be made can penetrate immediately into the fresh compost. Where a plant is flowering at this time of year, it should be repotted immediately after flowering.

A plant is in need of repotting when the leading pseudobulb has reached the rim of the pot and there is no room for future growth; or when the plant has become root-bound, and —in the case of Cymbidiums—when a plant has lifted itself above the rim of the pot. This could be six months after the last repotting, or more probably about two years. With Pleiones, Calanthes, Thunias and Phaius etc, which have a short fast growing season followed by a complete rest, it will be necessary to repot annually, using a rich compost of loam or peat plus sand or similar material mixed together with a liberal amount of dried cow manure in the base.

For repotting one should have handy a pair of sharp scissors, a stout potting stick, a sharp knife and a bucket for waste material such as old roots and compost. The potting bench should be prepared with a supply of ready-mixed compost, prepared a day or so earlier and in a damp condition, and sufficient clean crocks and pots of suitable size. Clay or plastic pots are suitable. It will have been seen that orchids breathe through their roots, and this they can easily do in a clay pot. Plastic pots are lighter, cleaner, and will require more drainage when used with economy composts.

An orchid plant can be completely repotted by cleaning out all old roots and compost, or merely 'dropped on', as is usual with young plants and seedlings. By this method the plant is potted on into a slightly larger pot without any disturbance to the existing root ball. The following lessons endeavour to describe these different methods in an easy style for a complete beginner to follow.

Potting Lesson 1. The straightforward dropping-on of a Cymbidium seedling into economy compost. As an example, a Cymbidium seedling, consisting of a strong single growth in a $2\frac{1}{2}$in pot, has been growing in economy compost for approximately twelve months. The plant has not been watered for the last few days, so that the compost is now on the dry side, and therefore decay will not result from damage to the roots. First hold the plant upside down and give the rim of the pot a few sharp taps against the potting bench to release the plant, revealing a healthy ball of solid white roots. Remove the crocks from in between the roots without disturbing the root ball. Take a pot approximately 4 inches in diameter (this is slightly larger than if one were potting in moss and fibre); place one large bevelled crock over the hole, which should be fairly large, and fill to about a quarter of the pot with crocks or brick rubble. Cover this with a thin layer of compost and place the plant in the pot. To judge the position, the base of the growth should be approximately ¼ inch below the rim of the pot. If this position is not achieved add or remove a little of the compost accordingly. Remove the plant and sprinkle a pinch of hoof and horn or bone meal, together with a small amount of dried cow manure, on the layer of compost.

Return the plant to the pot, holding it in position in the centre of the pot, and with one hand fill up the space with compost, firming it evenly down all around with a potting stick. Do this several times until the compost is within an inch of the rim, finishing with a level surface. The potting stick should be used in a downward movement, always against the rim of the pot and not applied directly against the roots. Finally surface off with a little chopped fresh sphagnum moss to bring the surface to within ¼ inch of the rim and level with the base of the plant, thus allowing for future watering.

The dropped-on plant should not be watered for a few days to give it a chance to settle down and any damaged roots to heal, but the foliage and surface of the compost may be lightly sprayed.

Potting Lesson 2. To repot a mature Cymbidium into economy compost. We have a Cymbidium in a 7 inch pot with three leafless pseudo-bulbs, four green pseudo-bulbs in leaf and one new growth approximately 3in high, which is against the rim of the pot, necessitating repotting. It has not been repotted for two years and is growing in economy compost. It is in an almost dry condition. The plant is first of all cleaned up by removing the stumps of discarded foliage from the older back bulbs, which are stripped down on each side of the bulb. The plant is knocked out of its pot as described above, care being taken not to damage the new growth. The pseudo-bulbs are large and we can therefore afford to remove the three leafless ones from the back of the plant. This is done by inserting a sharp knife in between the pseudo-bulbs and severing through the joining rhizome. These are separated and can be propagated providing they are hard and healthy. At the base of these pseudo-bulbs can be seen the dormant eye which will produce the new growth. Most of the old roots are cut away or trimmed, only sufficient being retained for anchorage in the new pot.

The bulbs are potted singly into 2—3in pots with pure fresh sphagnum moss only, potted loosely and not too deep, and placed in a propogating frame. Nine times out of ten they will start to grow and, encouraged by the fresh sphagnum moss will commence a new root system. Within a few months when the new growth is about 6 inches high, they can be removed into proper compost, and returned to the greenhouse. After eighteen months to two years, the plants will be self-supporting and the original back bulbs, which by this time will probably have shrivelled and dried up, may be removed. The pseudo-bulb should be removed at any time should it become soft and rotten.

To return to our main plant, remove the crocks and as much old compost as will come away, trimming back all dead roots, and live roots to a length of about 6in, otherwise they will snap off during potting. It may be necessary to remove as much as three-quarters of the root system, which in a healthy plant will do no harm, and will very quickly be made up. Try to finish up with a nice shape to the base of the plant, avoiding straggling bits of roots etc. Select the clean pot by trying the plant for size. The plant now has four pseudo-bulbs and the new growth and will probably go back into the original pot. With the back of the plant held against the rim of the pot, there should be just sufficient room between the front of the plant and the opposite edge of the pot for about a further two years growth.

Place a good layer of crocks in the bottom of the pot, covering them with a layer of compost. Sprinkle sufficient hoof and horn meal to cover a 50 pence piece and a few small pieces of dried cow manure on the compost. Onto this stand the Cymbidium. The layer of compost in the bottom should be sufficient to allow the plant to sit with the base of the new growth about $\frac{1}{2}$ inch below the rim of the pot. While holding the plant in position in one hand, fill in with compost all around. While in the previous lesson we had a solid ball of compost, here there is a loose entanglement of roots, and it is essential to work the compost well and evenly into these with the fingers, and firm down with the potting stick from the rim of the pot. To complete, surface with the chopped moss.

Where a plant has more than one leading growth and is growing in different directions, it may be possible to divide the plant into two, provided each section has at least three or four pseudo-bulbs and a lead. Each division is then potted up as described. It is always important that a plant should be firmly potted otherwise the vigorous root system of a Cymbidium will cause the plant to rise out of the pot. Finally always remember to replace the labels, and also label any back bulbs that were removed.

Potting Lesson 3. To repot a Cattleya into a 50-50 compost of moss and fibre. (The compost may include a little bracken, but certainly not loam or peat.) The plant is in a 5in pot and has one leafless pseudo-bulb and six pseudo-bulbs in leaf. The leading bulb has grown over the edge of the pot and its aerial roots have attached themselves to the outside of the pot. This plant has just completed its winter's rest and the new growth is about an inch high.

It is most important with Cattleyas to repot them at a time when the new growth is active but before the new roots are showing. This also applies to many other orchids which have a similar habit of growth and a definite resting period, unlike the Cymbidiums previously discussed, which are more or less continuous growing. The Cattleya is growing in a compost of moss and fibre and was last repotted three years ago. Earlier on in the year the rhizome joining the three oldest pseudo-bulbs was severed from the main plant, without any disturbance. A new growth is now showing on this severed division, which will be potted up separately and grown on. This is the

Page 53: (*left*) *Masdevallia coccinea*; (*below*) *Cymbidium* Rosanna 'Pinkie' FCC

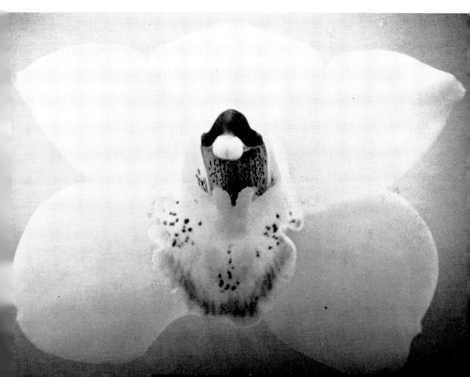

Page 54: (*above*) *Vanda tricolor;* (*below*) *Phalaenopsis equestris*

best method of propagating a Cattleya or allied plant, rather than cutting it at the time of repotting.

While the Cymbidium's thick fleshy roots tend to lift the plant out of its pot, the Cattleya roots will grip the inside and outside of the pot, making it difficult to remove. Damage to these roots will be unavoidable, but this is not important as the roots will be severely trimmed back to within a few inches of the rhizome. These will start to grow again after repotting and form a secondary root system. The important roots are those which will shortly come from the new growth. The main plant will now go back, probably into the same sized pot, with sufficient room being left for a further two to three years growth, while a suitably sized smaller pot is selected for the division. Swift drainage is most important for Cattleyas and therefore more crocks are used than for Cymbidiums, the pot being crocked up to about half way; if half-pots are used, which are most suitable for these orchids, less crocks will be required. Place a layer of compost over the crocks and add the hoof and horn meal.

Position the plant with the oldest bulb against the rim of the pot and the new growth just about level with the proposed surface of the compost. To obtain this it may be necessary with some varieties to bury a portion of the rhizome and older bulbs, which is quite in order provided the lead sits on the compost in an upright position. With the plant held thus, fill in with compost all around the plant, firming down with the potting stick until approximately 2 inches from the rim of the pot, and the plant should stand erect of its own accord.

With this open and springy compost it is essential to get a firm even surface to allow for swift drainage, and this is done in the following manner. The compost is inserted in wads which are made up by taking a small handful of compost and tearing it in half, placing the two halves together and repeating the process once or twice, thus bringing the compost into upright layers. Practice makes for good judgement as to the

D

size of the wad needed which will, of course, vary with the space to be filled. While the compost is held in one hand trim off the top with a pair of scissors before inserting it into the pot, which is done with a twisting movement down and towards the plant, pushing with the potting stick at the pot rim. Repeat this action and continue working around the plant, placing each wad tightly against the previous one until potting is completed. The surface should now be just below the rim of the pot. If preferred, the trimming may be left until the surfacing is completed, provided care is taken to avoid snipping the plant. Surfacing should not be difficult, and once understood is easily mastered. However, there is nothing like seeing the job demonstrated for oneself, and a visit to an orchid nursery for this purpose is always of great benefit.

The division should be labelled and potted in a similar way, not in pure moss since it has already begun to grow. Young seedlings being dropped on in moss and fibre would be potted in the same way, without disturbing the existing ball of compost. This method of potting will also apply to all orchids growing in this compost.

Growing on Wood. In a small amateur's greenhouse where there is a constant problem of finding sufficient space to accommodate one's ever-increasing orchid collection, and where a mixed variety of plants is grown, it can be of great advantage to grow suitable species on wood suspended from the roof. This saves valuable staging space and has the added attraction of allowing one to watch the plants more easily, and especially the long aerial roots growing.

The species most suited to this type of culture are those with long creeping rhizomes such as several of the Bulbophyllums and Cirrhopetalums, one or two Oncidiums, including *O. flexuosum, Miltonia flavescens* and *Epigeneium amplum,* whose bulbs appear at intervals of about 6 inches or so along the rhizome—it would indeed be an impossibilty to get such a plant as this into an ordinary pot! Wood culture also suits species with an upward climbing habit as, for example. *Maxillaria tenuifolia, Oncidium papilio, Rodrequezia venusta, Laelia anceps, Epidendrum polybulbon* and several of the Vandas. Then we must not forget the hanging type of plant which may include *Dendrobium falconeri* and *D. primulinum*, the Scuticarias, *Epidendrum medusae* and *E. falcatum* as a few examples. These are also among the type of orchids which will benefit from the amount of extra light they will receive in their position close to the glass, although at the same time it must be remembered that too much sun will cause the plants to dry out very quickly, and they must be kept regularly sprayed.

More or less anything that is handy will make a suitable home for the right species. Cork bark is attractive to look at, or any bark for that matter, the rougher the surface the better, to enable the roots to get a better grip into the bark when establishing themselves. Half-coconut shells can be used, hung on their sides, with drainage holes drilled in the bottom. Blocks of tree fern can be purchased and used as they are, with no compost being added to them. There is sufficient food in the slab to sustain a plant for several years. Wooden rafts and baskets are easily made; even old dried sheep skulls can be used and they make an ideal, if somewhat unusual anchorage for an orchid, with again a certain amount of food value to be found by the plant in the bone.

Where there is sufficient room at one end of the greenhouse a branch or bough from an oak or apple tree can look very attractive, to which can be attached a variety of epiphytes, placing the species in the axils of the branches, where they will very quickly become naturalised. For this purpose one can use species whose flowers have a pendent habit, such as *Coelogyne flaccida* or *C. massangeana, Cymbidium devonianum, Oncidium concolor, Aërides fieldingii* among others and, if carefully placed, Stanhopeas. Perhaps something like *Epidendrum radicans* or *Angraecum eichlerianum* could be used coming up from the ground to cover the lower trunk.

If there is no room in your greenhouse for such a bough, try attaching a piece of bamboo trellis against a wall, onto which the species on bark can be placed.

Where a species in need of repotting is being taken from a pot to be placed on bark, first remember to bore a hole in the top of the wood and place a piece of wire through it for hanging. The piece of wood should be somewhat larger than the overall size of the plant, with plenty of room for future growth. All old compost should be removed from the plant, also any dead roots, with live ones being trimmed to about 3 to 4 inches. Osmunda fibre and sphagnum moss should be used for the compost, but not mixed together. Place a suitable piece or clump of unpulled fibre on the wood, and on top of this a little fresh moss with plenty of live green heads. Or if preferred, especially if the fibre being used is a nice looking piece with a rhizome in it, put the moss on first, leaving the heads to protrude from the edges of the fibre. In either case, with correct spraying, it will soon begin to grow and establish itself. There is no need to cover the whole surface of the wood with the compost; just use sufficient to be covered by the underside of the plant. If it is a long thin plant, use long thin pieces of fibre to match, and so on.

The plant should be placed so that there is plenty of room for future growth, bearing in mind which way the plant is growing. The plant will remain on this wood for several years, and it should only be necessary to place further pieces of fibre and moss under or in front of the leading growths each year or so.

Where one is using a basket, coconut shell or sheep's skull, the plant is potted into the hole or cavity in the same way as when being potted into a pot, using the moss and fibre mixed together in the usual way.

For attaching the plant to the bark, use nylon fishing line; this is very strong, and is hardly noticeable when pulled tight. When winding the line around the plant and bark, care should be taken to place the line in between the pseudo-bulbs where it will not cut into the tough woody rhizome, and avoid cutting across a pseudo-bulb or, worse, new growth. This line should be pulled as tight as possible, so as to give the plant as much anchorage as possible before its own roots have adhered to the wood.

If the plants are well sprayed and not allowed to dry out, as they will very quickly, they should have established themselves firmly to the wood within twelve months, with plenty of active aerial roots being made from the new growths. If a plant does not keep sufficiently wet with spraying, a dip in the water tank will ensure a thorough wetting.

Five

Pests and Diseases

By their very nature orchids are an undesirable host for most pests such as attack other greenhouse plants. The number we have to be concerned with is very small, although these can be a considerable nuisance if allowed to remain unchecked. Bearing in mind that prevention is better than cure, all orchid growers should make a routine job of fumigating, using aerosols and spraying their plants against the most common pests mentioned here. The insecticide should be regularly changed as the pests can build up an immunity to certain chemicals over a period of time. For most pests there are a number of different controls available on the market today, and strict adherence to the maker's instructions is always important. To avoid spotting or discolouring, any blooms should be removed from the greenhouse before fumigating.

Cleanliness in the greenhouse combined with regular inspection of the plants is most important. All old leaves and any decaying matter, such as old flowers, should be thrown away outside and not under the staging where they will harbour pests and spread disease.

There are two ways in which pests and diseases may enter the greenhouse. Firstly there are the kinds which are indigenous to orchids and these can be introduced into the collection with new plants that are brought in. Secondly, there are the common or garden pests which enter the greenhouse of their own accord from outside surroundings, particularly in the spring and autumn months when they are attracted and encouraged to breed by the warmth of the greenhouse.

Red Spider Mite. This is neither a spider, nor is it red! It is a mite, pale orange-yellow in colour, only just discernible with the naked eye—a magnifying glass is necessary for real study. It should be looked for on the underside of the leaves where it will breed in great numbers in a very short period, the young being hatched from eggs. In large colonies this mite will protect itself with a very fine web which is most easily seen on the stems of flower buds. This pest enjoys a hot, dry atmosphere and will attack the leaves and buds on Cymbidiums quicker than anything. On Cymbidium buds this pest will damage the surface of the sepals, causing them to twist and the flower will open prematurely and be deformed. In bad cases the bud will turn yellow and drop off. Red spider will also attack the softer-leaved Dendrobiums and Odontoglossums. Its presence can be detected by white papery patches, caused by the drying up of the leaf cells.

Red spider prefers the undersides of leaves because this is usually a dry safe position. It is therefore a good preventative against this pest to spray the undersides of the leaves with water when damping down during the summer months. The best method of control is by fumigation, using Azobenzene once a month, or where a bad attack has been discovered every seven to ten days. Malathion can also be used as an insecticide spray or dip. Spraying can, however, cause harm to buds, which are more delicate, and buds should therefore be fumigated.

Scale Insects. There are many different types of scale insects which settle down in one place and cover themselves in a scaly membrane. This is usually whitish in colour and in one type accompanied by a white woolly substance not to be confused with mealy bug. Scale is found mostly on Cattleyas and Cymbidiums, also on a number of the species orchids. On Cymbidiums it is usually the harder type of scale which is found on the leaves and bulbs. When removed it leaves a permanent reminder in the form of a small yellow or white patch. On Cattleyas it can build up into large colonies of a softer type, where it will cover the bulbs and rhizomes underneath the sheaths, destroying dormant growths and new root tips, and eventually leading to the destruction of the plant. New additions to one's collection should always be checked for scale by peeling back the covering sheaths.

This pest is too persistent and vigorous for fumigation to have very much effect. The best form of control is the use of Malathion solution in a bucket. The plant is then dipped up to the rim of the pot and the pest brushed away with a small stiff paint brush after the sheaths have been removed from the plant. Methylated spirit can also be used for brushing away the pest.

It is advisable to place all affected plants together to enable repeated checks to be made; this pest may return several times before being finally stamped out.

Mealy Bug. This small insect is another sap-sucking pest which lives under a white mealy powder and is more manoeuvrable than scale. Like scale it is usually introduced on dirty plants coming into the greenhouse. Mealy bug, which can greatly weaken a plant if left unchecked, is usually found in the axils of the leaves of most orchids. Control is the same as for scale.

Slugs and Snails. These are too well known to any gardener to require description, but are nevertheless dangerous pests. It is unfortunate that the warm, moist conditions in the orchid house are ideally suited to slugs and snails and measures must be continually taken to control them.

While they may avoid the harder-leaved plants, they will attack and eat tender young growths and roots tips. They are particularly fond of flower-spikes and buds, and can eat their way right through a flower-spike overnight. They will also eat their way into a mature pseudo-bulb which, unless detected in good time, they may completely hollow out. A routine job should be made of regularly watering the plants, benches and paths etc, with liquid slug-killer and liberally distributing slug-pellets. Where flower-spikes are concerned, it is a good protective measure to place a band of cotton wool around the base of the spike and supporting cane which, provided it is kept dry, no slug or snail can cross.

Where a pseudo-bulb has been badly damaged, it is important to treat it as soon as discovered before any decay can set up. The hole must first be cleaned out with the sharp point of a penknife, removing any secretion from the wound, and then be thoroughly dried with cotton wool. The hole is then dusted liberally with powdered charcoal, sulphur or captan. The plant should be kept dry for a few days, above all keeping water away from the affected area.

A small brownish snail, commonly known as the garlic snail, can become a great nuisance among young seedlings, where it appears to be unconcerned by liquid slug-killers or slug-bait. A good old-fashioned remedy here is to place thin slices of apple or potato on the surface of the compost. By the following morning the snails will be found to have congregated on the underside of the slices, which should be removed after two or three days before moulds appear.

Greenfly. This is only too common a pest, and often met in the greenhouse. Greenfly will come in from outside and attack tender buds and new growths, where they will breed rapidly and set up large colonies if allowed to. Upon detection they may be wiped from a Cymbidium spike with no apparent signs of damage to the buds. But later, when the flower opens, damaged tissue will appear as very small lumps on the sepals. For control, fumigation with a BHC aerosol, or the use of impregnated plastic strips, are recommended. Spraying with certain insecticides should be avoided as these can cause further damage to buds and flowers. Some types of aphids are very resistant to control, and therefore different remedies should be applied from time to time.

Ants. These are comparatively harmless in the greenhouse, but they will encourage and spread greenfly, and are therefore not to be encouraged. Various ant-killing materials are available.

Thrips. Like red spider these are too small to be seen easily with the naked eye. They are sap-sucking insects and it is usually the damage caused which is noticed first, in the form of semi-transparent pin-holes on the foliage of most orchids, especially on new growths of Odontoglossums, Cymbidiums, etc, and on their flowers. Control is best effected with Malathion in a spray or fumigant, repeated as necessary.

Springtails. These are small, grey, wingless insects, and very fast-moving. They can be found on the staging, in upturned pots, or among the crocks and compost of plants. In small quantities springtails are insufficient to do any real harm. However, among seedlings they cause greater damage by breaking down the compost and even damaging the roots of the youngest plants. Springtails breed in the compost, thus making fumigation ineffective as a control. The best method is to give any plants a thorough watering with BHC solution, at the same time watering the staging.

Moss Flies. These small blackish flies can be seen flying around just above the surface of the compost. While the flies do no harm themselves, the larvae, hatched from eggs laid in the compost will feed on the live moss, thus breaking down the compost in a similar way to springtails. Where a bad infestation is present, the whole surface is devoid of any moss and becomes badly clogged, making the passage of water very difficult, so that from the surface a plant will appear to be wet enough, while the underneath will be bone dry. When the moss has been destroyed the attention of the larvae will turn to small seedlings and they will eat into the base of the plants, destroying the root systems.

Control is not easy, since the flies breed and increase at an alarming rate in high temperatures. The adults can be killed by fumigation and aerosols, but within a day or two a second generation will have emerged to lay further eggs, and so on. Fumigations are therefore necessary in rapid succession to break up their life-cycle. Like the springtails the larvae can be killed by adding BHC insecticide when watering, after which the dead larvae will come to the surface.

Other Pests. Apart from the foregoing there are a number of other pests which may occasionally crop up in an orchid house, such as woodlice, encouraged in a dirty greenhouse by rotting leaves, etc, left under the staging. In old greenhouses and conservatories cockroaches and crickets may appear, and can be destructive to flowers.

Mice. Mice are attracted into the greenhouse by the warmth, mostly during the autumn and winter, and will make their home in any empty flower pots, boxes, etc, stored near heating systems or hot-water pipes. They will eat flowers, buds, root tips, seedlings and even gnaw at pseudo-bulbs, doing an amazing amount of damage in one night. Although not frequently met with in the greenhouse mice must not be underestimated. They are easily controlled by setting traps or placing poison immediately they are discovered.

Bees. In the early spring when there is a show of orchids in bloom, spells of bright weather will bring out the first bees, at a time when few, if any, flowers are to be found in the garden outside. The bees are quickly attracted to the orchids, where in a few minutes they will have pollinated any number of flowers. Instead of lasting for many weeks in perfection, the flowers will turn red and within a couple of days collapse, as fertilisation takes place. It is usually the large and beautiful bumble bee which fits perfectly into a Cymbidium flower and does more harm than the smaller honey bee. The only way to ensure that bees are kept out of the greenhouse is to cover the ventilator openings with a fine mesh or net curtaining, and make sure there are no other small openings.

Diseases. Orchids, especially the Cymbidiums, are rather prone to getting black tips or odd black marks on their foliage. Provided this remains on the older foliage and is not excessive there is usually nothing to worry about. For neatness, black tips can be trimmed back with a pair of scissors. During the autumn most orchids will quite naturally discard some, if not all, of their foliage; therefore yellow leaves on the oldest pseudo-bulbs at this time of the year are to be expected.

Such black markings must not be confused with what is known as virus disease, or Cymbidium mosaic. Although in recent years a closer understanding of virus in orchids has been reached, a great deal is still to be learnt. It is generally believed that some viruses are present in most plants, but remain undetected where healthy conditions prevail. Prolonged exposure to cold, combined with high humidity, gross overfeeding or overwatering, and general bad culture will encourage trouble.

There appear to be quite a number of viruses which affect all genera of orchids. In Cymbidiums, virus disease appears as a white flecking in the new growth, intermittent along the length of the leaf, in bad cases forming a mosaic pattern. As the foliage ages, these markings turn black, disfiguring the foliage and causing premature yellowing of the remainder of the leaf and its subsequent shedding. In other orchids virus will take on a similar appearance. In very bad cases it can kill a plant.

There is no known cure for virus, but where a plant is mildly affected, good culture and a slightly higher temperature will assist in retarding its progress. Virus can be spread by practically all the pests previously described, as well as by knives used for cutting leaves or flower spikes, or roots at repotting time. Therefore it is essential in the interests of the plants to keep pests and diseases to a minimum, and to sterilise any cutting instrument used by passing through a flame.

Blemishes. A number of blemishes may appear on the foliage of orchids in the form of black spots, markings or rings, and soft bulbs on mature plants. These are caused by cultural faults rather than a disease or a virus. Miltonias, for example, are particularly prone to black spots on their foliage owing to their delicate nature. The answer is usually to allow more ventilation and a slightly drier atmosphere, which will prevent the spots from spreading, although those already present will not disappear. These troubles usually reach their peak during the autumn and winter, when a correct balance between the temperature and humidity is most important. This subject is discussed more fully under 'Culture' (see p 31).

Six

Seed Sowing and Raising of Seedlings

There is nothing to compare with the sheer thrill of flowering an orchid which has been raised and lovingly grown in one's own greenhouse. Today, many amateurs can, and do, produce their own hybrids. Although it means several years before seeing the fruits of one's work, it is nevertheless amply rewarding.

Before venturing into hybridising, certain rules of nature must be understood. While with orchids it is possible to make bigeneric and even multigeneric hybrids as in no other flower, the beginner would be wise to experiment with one genus only, which will ensure that the parents are compatible. For example, cross an Odontoglossum with another Odontoglossum. This genus may also be crossed with an Oncidium, for these two orchids are closely allied genera belonging to the same sub-tribe, and will produce a bigeneric hybrid, if the cross is successful. It is, however, impossible to hybridise from two members of completely different tribes, such as an Odontoglossum and a Vanda.

Two fresh flowers should be carefully chosen for their good qualities such as colour, shape, size and habit of spike, with a view to combining the best qualities from both flowers. The breeder should decide which plant will contribute the pollen and which plant bear the pod. The strongest plant should be chosen for the latter, bearing in mind that the pod will take approximately nine to twelve months to ripen and the plant should not require repotting before that time.

The unwanted pollen from the first flower of the pod or female plant is removed by inserting a pointed matchstick under the pollen cap and lifting upwards. The cap will fall away leaving the pollinia attached to the end of the matchstick by the viscid disc.

From the pollen parent or male half of the cross, select a pollen-mass which is a clear yellow and which has not been infected by mildew. This is gently pressed onto the stigma of the female flower where it will readily adhere to the glutinous surface.

There is one exception to this method, with the Paphiopedilums and allied genera. In these orchids the pollen-masses, which are of an orange-brown colour, are situated one on each side of the column without the protection of a pollen cap. To fertilise these flowers, a square must be cut out from the hindpart of the pouch to enable one to place the pollen upon the stigma.

It is not necessary to use the pollen collected immediately; in some genera it can be stored for several months, thus enabling the hybridist to cross two plants which may be flowering at different times of the year. For this use a test tube, first filled to about a quarter with silica gel crystals (to keep the pollen dry) and covered with a small wad of cotton wool. On top of this the pollen is placed; the test tube is then tightly stoppered. It should then be labelled with the plant's name and date and kept in the cool and dark.

Returning to the pollinated plant, make a note of the cross and date of pollination, preferably placing a coded label on the plant. The plant should then be placed in a shady position out of the direct sun. The reaction of the fertilised flower will be swift and noticeable within a day or two as the end of the column swells and closes around the pollen.

With Cymbidiums in particular the lip will go through the

most beautiful shades of red. This precedes the collapse of the flower. Except in the Paphiopedilums, where the flower will drop off of its own accord, the petals should be trimmed and dusted with sulphur to prevent mildew appearing. The pollen tubes will quickly travel down the column and into the stem at the back of the flower where the ovaries will begin to swell, and as fertilisation takes place a large seed pod will start its development. The remaining flowers may then be removed from the spike.

For the next ten to twelve months, while the seed pod is ripening, no special care or attention is required, but it is advisable not to allow the plant to flower again during this period. Any time after nine months, depending upon the genus, the pod should be examined daily. At the first sign of a slight yellowing, and before the end begins to split, the pod should be cut from the plant. The end of the pod is cut off, and the seed shaken out onto a piece of absorbent paper: filter paper or blotting paper is ideal. The pod may be found to be completely empty, or it may contain many thousands of extremely fine seeds, usually a lovely pale yellow, which should fall freely from the pod.

The seed should be sown as fresh as possible, although if necessary it may be stored, wrapped in the filter paper, in the same way as the pollen, although it will deteriorate the longer it is stored.

There are two ways open for the amateur to grow the seed —the natural method, and the artificial method of culturing them in a bottle. Which method to use should have been decided well in advance of harvesting the seed. All orchids are possessed by a mycorrhiza, which is a microscopic fungus. It assists the orchid by releasing trace elements in the soil. Without this mycorrhiza it is very difficult for the seeds to germinate and grow.

The mycorrhiza infects not only the orchid, but also abounds in the compost. It is for this reason that seeds are sown on the compost of a host plant.

Page 71:
(*above*) *Cymbidium devonianum;*
(*left*) *Coelogyne ochracea*

Page 72 :
(*above*) *Dendrobium infundibulum;*

(*right*) *Laelia pumila*

SEED SOWING

The Natural Method

The natural method is by far the easiest for the amateur, particularly where only a limited number of plants are required. It is still widely used today, particularly in the culture of Paphiopedilums. The foster parent should be of the same genus as the seed, and the plant should have been potted for about twelve months, showing a good green head of moss on the surface of the compost. The whole surface should be trimmed as evenly as possible, and the plant thoroughly watered before scattering the seed over the surface.

The future watering of the plant should be done with great care so as not to wash the seeds over the edge. It is best done by standing the plant in a bucket of water, with the water just below the rim of the pot, and allowing the water to soak up to the surface. The compost should never be allowed to become dry at any time. Due to the affinity which will be built up between the host plant's mycorrhiza and the seed, the young seedlings will begin to grow. It may take many weeks or even months before any sign of movement is seen, during which time slugs, moss flies, etc, must be kept at bay and the plant kept in a warm and shady position. The surface moss should not be allowed to become too prolific so as to suffocate the seedlings.

When the seedlings are established and large enough they may be removed from the host plant and potted up on their own. This should be done by knocking the plant out of its pot and separating the compost from the seedlings. This operation should be tackled in the spring, when the seedlings have the summer growing months ahead of them.

By the above method only a very small percentage of the seed sown will germinate and grow; but for the small amateur this will be more than sufficient for his needs.

The Artificial Method

While for many years the hybridist was working with host plants, several botanists were busily engaged trying to isolate the various orchid fungi. This was only partially successful, but led to a better understanding of the requirements of the seed for germination. In 1922 Dr Knudson developed several formulae based on the nutrients produced by the fungi. The most important of these is known as 'Knudson Formula C' and is still widely used as a basis. The ingredients, when mixed with agar and sterilised in flasks, will set in the form of a jelly on which the seed can be sown. Provided the few basic rules of hygiene are understood every seed stands a good chance of germinating by this method.

Asymbiotic culture, as it is known, is within the reach of any amateur, and the various chemicals required are easily obtainable from a chemist. Alternatively, the prepared medium may be purchased ready for use. The following items of equipment will first be required.

One pair of accurate metric scales
One double boiler
One litre measure
One pH soil testing outfit
One 100cc measure resistant to heat
Ten 500cc flasks or similar bottles that will stand sterilisation, such as milk bottles
Ten rubber stoppers with glass tubing, or cotton wool stoppers (non-absorbent) to fit flasks
One autoclave or pressure cooker
One piece of wood 40in long and approx 1in square for laying out bottles
One packet filter papers
One glass funnel
One glass stirring rod
One glass 5cc vial
One piece of platinum wire, 1½in long, mounted in a length

of glass tubing 10in long
   One pair rubber gloves
   One bottle potassium hydroxide
   One bottle hydrochloric acid N.10
   One jar calcium hypochlorite
   One gallon distilled water
   Fifteen grams agar

Where the medium is to be prepared rather than purchased ready mixed, here is the Knudson Formula C. The chemicals should be weighed out with the utmost accuracy, for any discrepancy in the proportions may be disastrous for the seedlings.

Knudson Formula 'C'

Chemical	Symbol	Amount	
Calcium nitrate	$Ca(NO_3)_2.4H_2O$	1.00	gram
Monobasic potassium phosphate	KH_2PO_4	0.25	gram
Magnesium sulphate	$MgSO_4.7H_2O$	0.25	gram
Ammonium sulphate	$(NH_4)_2SO_4$	0.50	gram
Sucrose	$C_{12}H_{22}O_{11}$	20.00	grams
Ferrous sulphate	$FeSO_4.7H_2O$	0.025	gram
Manganese sulphate	$MnSO_4.4H_2O$	0.0075	gram

To prepare the medium pour a litre of distilled water into the double boiler and start to warm. Add each chemical one at a time plus the fifteen grams of agar and stir in with the glass rod until the whole is thoroughly dissolved and quite hot. Remove a sample of the mixture and check the pH (hydrogen-ion concentration). The sample should be tested with the colour soil testing outfit following the instructions supplied with it. Should this turn yellow as is usual, the solution is too alkaline, and this should be counteracted by the addition of a few drops of hydrochloric acid N.10 to the solution and thoroughly stirred. Test a small quantity again until the orange colour is obtained, indicating a pH of about 5.0 which is correct. Should the test turn red the medium is too acid, in which case add a few drops of potassium hydroxide to obtain the orange state.

The solution is now ready to be measured out, pouring approximately 100ccs into each 500cc flask or appropriate bottle. Any kind of bottle is suitable provided it will withstand sterilising and have a sufficiently wide neck to work through. Each flask should be tightly stoppered. Either use a rubber bung with one hole filled with a glass tube, which in turn is packed with cotton wool. Alternatively, cotton wool stoppers can be made by tightly rolling a 2in strip of non-absorbent cotton wool approximately 12in long, which should firmly fit the neck of the bottle when screwed in.

When the flasks have been filled and tightly stoppered, they are ready for sterilising by placing in the pressure cooker or autoclave at a pressure of 15lb for 20 minutes, or they may be boiled in a large saucepan for the same length of time.

After sterilising, the flasks are removed, using an oven cloth, and laid on their sides with the necks resting on the wooden rack. Adjust the level so that the liquid is not lying too close to the neck of the flask. Alternatively, the flasks may be left upright, which is sometimes preferred. Allow the flasks to set overnight before attempting to sow them.

Although not necessary, it is interesting at this point to check the viability of the seed. First place a single drop of water onto a microscope slide and sprinkle a few seeds on it and cover with another slide. Examine under a microscope with a magnification of 100. It will be seen that each seed is surrounded by an open-work husk, rather like a string shopping bag, in the centre of which is the embryo seed. Under the microscope this appears as a dark circular shape. This means that the seed is fertile; any husks which do not contain this embryo are not fertile. By doing a rough count one can estimate the expectancy of the seed.

It is now necessary to sterilise the seed before introducing it to the prepared flasks. The air is full of microscopic spores and the moment the seed leaves the capsule it becomes contaminated. If sown on to the agar in this condition moulds will rapidly grow and expand to cover the whole surface within the flask within a few days. If the seed is taken straight from the pod it will be naturally moist and when placed in the sterilising solution will quickly become saturated. However, where the seed has been stored, wrapped in the filter paper, it will be quite dry; and some difficulty may be encountered in thoroughly wetting it. In this case a single drop of washing-up liquid will act as a wetting agent and help to break up the air bubbles surrounding the seed. The easiest way to introduce the liquid soap is by placing a smear on the end of the cork before inserting it into the vial.

If, after taking these extra precautions, every flask still produces a mould, and the moulds are identical, this could mean that the seed is contaminated by an extremely virile fungus, which may have attacked the seed before it left the pod. In cases such as this, where contamination of the seed is suspected, take a fresh portion of the seed, and pour it into the vial containing a quarter of a teaspoon of sugar dissolved in distilled water. This is placed in a temperature of 70°F for 24 hours. The effect of this treatment will be to start the spores growing, making them easier to kill without harming the seed. The seed is then transferred with a wire loop to the sterilising solution.

To sterilise the seed, first weigh 10 grams of calcium hypochlorite and dissolve thoroughly in 140ccs of distilled water. This solution is filtered through a funnel lined with a filter paper and sufficient of the clear solution taken to three-quarters fill a 5cc vial. This must be used immediately as it quickly begins to lose its strength. Add a small portion of the seed to the vial which is corked and shaken vigorously and continuously for about five minutes. This will break up the minute air bubbles that surround each seed. The sterilised seed is now ready for sowing.

There are a number of methods of maintaining strict hygiene during this operation but one of the easiest and satisfactory methods for an amateur to use is to work inside a simple glove box. This is easily made on a wooden frame covered in polythene, leaving two holes which fit tightly round the wrists, through which it is possible to work with gloved hands. Into the sowing frame is placed all the equipment required: the flasks, the vial containing the seed, the platinum loop for sowing, a saucer full of the filtered calcium hypochlorite, and a swab of cotton wool.

Wearing the rubber gloves, swab around the inside of the box, carefully wiping all surfaces including the flasks and implements to be used. Having done this one should now be able to work through the holes provided, knowing that the box is thoroughly clean.

Wipe the glass rod and platinum wire loop with a cotton swab and place in the saucer. Swab the stopper and neck of the first flask and remove the stopper and place it in the saucer. Dipping the wire loop into the seed, which will have risen to the top of the vial, extract a small portion at a time in the loop. Starting at the back of the flask, work towards the neck, passing the loop slowly over the jelly so as to spread the seed evenly and as thinly as possible, bearing in mind that every seed has an equal chance of germinating.

Restopper the flask and repeat with the next, until the job is completed. The flasks should be kept level at all times.

It is difficult to advise the exact amount of seed to be put into each flask; this depends so much upon the viability of the seed and the type of cross made, also whether reflasking is to be attempted at a later date. The beginner should experiment by sowing some flasks more thinly than others and observing the results. With practice, the time the flask remains open can be cut down, thus reducing the danger of contamination.

If preferred, the sowing may be carried out over a bowl of

steaming water, working to the above procedure. Care must be exercised not to disturb the air more than possible, and not to breath upon the open flasks and the work in progress.

Where cotton wool bungs have been used, after sowing these should be covered with polythene held in place with rubber bands, or alternatively tin-foil covers be made as an added precaution against contamination.

The flasks should be labelled with the name of the parents and placed in a humid propagating frame with a minimum temperature of not less than 60°F (16°C) and shaded from the direct sunlight. The necks of the flasks should be rested upon a 1in rack to keep the agar level.

If, after a few days, a mould appears in any one of the flasks, regrettably nothing can be done about it, except to repeat the process endeavouring to be more hygienic. If all goes well within the flasks, the seed will swell into large, green protocorms, prior to the development of leaves and roots. How long this will take again depends upon the genus. Odontoglossums will turn green within a few weeks while other orchids may take several months to reach this stage.

Reflasking. From now onwards there will be very little attention required by the flasks, and the less handling they receive the better. The seedlings will remain in the flasks for approximately twelve months, by which time they will have grown into sturdy little plants. After about four months, however, when the plants are still very small, they may be reflasked to allow more room to each seedling. The new flasks can contain a 'boosted' agar, which would be too strong for sowing, but will greatly increase the seedlings' vigour at this stage of their growth.

For those who wish to attempt reflasking further flasks should be prepared in the foregoing manner with the addition, before sterilising, of a portion of banana. The banana should not be too ripe and cut into slices $\frac{1}{4}$ inch thick. These slices are cut into two, and one half is added to each flask. Other fruit juices may be used, such as tomato or grape, but we have found that the banana is the most nutritious.

After the jelly has set the transflasking is carried out in the seed frame previously used, under the same strict hygienic conditions. The old and new flasks are placed side by side and both stoppers removed after throughly swabbing everything with the calcium hypochlorite solution. A bottle will be required containing distilled water which has been previously sterilised by boiling for twenty minutes and being allowed to cool. A long-handled spoon will be needed for picking up the seedlings; it must first be sterilised with the solution and rinsed in the bottle containing the sterilised distilled water. This is important as any contact between the solution and the seedlings will result in the plants being burnt.

By drawing the spoon across the agar, a few of the seedlings may be scooped up and transferred immediately to the new flask, spreading them as thinly as possible on the surface of the agar until it is evenly covered. The stopper is then replaced and the operation repeated with the next flask. The contents of one flask may make up to six new ones. The seedlings must be handled as little as possible, as they are very easily bruised. Any seedlings that are not in an upright position when reflasked will very quickly right themselves of their own accord. It cannot be stressed enough that hygiene when reflasking is even more important than when sowing, as the flasks will remain open for a longer period and direct sterilising of the plants is impossible.

If all goes well, rapid progress will be made by the seedlings, and during the following spring months they may be removed and potted up.

Care of the seedlings from flasks. The seedlings may be put into community pots consisting of finely chopped osmunda fibre and sphagnum moss, or trays of sphagnum peat and sand, depending upon the genera. Cymbidium seedlings will grow and thrive very well in a compost of peat and sand, either in trays or beds, depending upon the room available, and the quantity of seedlings to be pricked out. Oncidiums, Dendrobiums, and other fine-rooting orchids settle down and grow better in community pots of moss and fibre.

The community pots or trays should be prepared at least two to three weeks before they are to be used, to give the compost time to settle, and the surface moss time to grow. When preparing community pots, a $2\frac{1}{2}$in half-pot is most suitable and this should be well crocked. The compost may consist of approximately two parts osmunda fibre to three parts of sphagnum moss, the latter to be fresh and green, and perfectly clean. This moss and fibre should be finely chopped and thoroughly mixed together. After putting a small pinch of hoof and horn meal in the base, the compost should be placed in the pot in upright layers, using the same method as employed when surfacing a larger plant, only in this case one wad of compost should be made to fit into the pot neatly and, most important, with the same firmness all around the pot.

The surface is very important to make easy insertion of the seedlings possible, and it should be well trimmed with a sharp pair of scissors until it is smooth and slightly bevelled, with the edge just below the rim of the pot to allow for future watering.

When the pot is completed it can be watered immediately, preferably with a liquid slug-killer; if of the correct firmness, the water will run swiftly through the compost, and not take several seconds to drain as we like to see with mature plants.

Where a compost of peat and sand is to be used, it is better to use wooden or plastic trays, or possibly make up a small bed on the bench. In either case, good drainage is again essential, with a liberal layer of crocks, on top of which should be placed a thin layer of compost, equal portions of sphagnum peat and sand, and on top of this a light sprinkling of dried, powdered cow manure, and hoof and horn meal, together with a little BHC powder, which later on will help to keep away any moss flies. On top of this is placed the remainder of the compost until the whole is about one to two inches deep: since most orchids are surface rooting, it is not necessary to make it any deeper. On the surface, sprinkle a little very finely chopped moss; this will grow, giving a good green and healthy surface to the tray.

After two to three weeks these containers are ready for use, and any large heads of moss that may have grown should be trimmed back, as too much growth of moss may choke the seedlings.

The seedlings should be carefully removed from the flask with the aid of a thin wire hook, having first poured a little water at greenhouse temperature into the flask, which will make it easier to remove the seedlings. These should be taken out root first and placed in a bowl of water, also at greenhouse temperature. To this can be added a fungicide such as captan with some BHC solution as a precaution against damping off and moss flies respectively. It is important to wash all agar from around the base and roots of the seedlings as this will only encourage moulds to appear.

Where the seedlings are to be placed into the trays of peat and sand, which should be lightly watered beforehand, it is an easy matter to make a straight furrow just deep enough for the seedlings to be placed in; they can be placed fairly close together, with any long roots carefully tucked in. Any roots that have become broken or damaged are better removed. The seedlings should be handled with a blunted pair of forceps, and picked up gently at the base of the plant rather than by the tip of the leaf. When one row has been completed, using two fingers work down the row, pressing the compost in around the plants, until they are sitting firmly on the surface, not too deep and not too high. The rows can be about two to three inches apart, depending upon the room available.

Where community pots are being used, there is, perhaps, a little more skill and patience required. Using a thin, sharp potting stick, make an insertion in the compost, which should be quite easy if the pot has been prepared as previously mentioned, into which the seedling is placed. When the potting stick is removed the compost will spring back into place, supporting the seedling as it does so. In this manner the pot can be filled with ten to fifteen seedlings, depending upon their size, including around the rim of the pot. As long roots can sometimes be difficult to tuck in, reserve the rim for any extra long-rooted seedlings. If any roots are damaged in this process, it is better to cut them off, and try again.

It is important with these little plants to handle them as little as possible; a plant leaning over a bit is better left alone, rather than risk damaging it while trying to alter its position. The more a seedling is handled at this stage the greater the risk of damaging it. Any inadvertent damage will show up clearly within a few days, when the seedlings should be removed at once. Each day the seedlings can be checked for any damping off, and any such seedlings removed from the pot. After a few days the seedlings will need watering, and this is best done by submerging the pot almost to the rim, and allowing the water to soak up to the surface, avoiding any water getting onto the plants themselves. The easiest way to water the trays without washing the seedlings away is with a rosed watering can, and a fine sunny morning should be selected, when the foliage will dry off quickly.

It will be found that the community pots will require more frequent watering than the trays. In either case, the seedlings should never be allowed to become completely dry, but kept at a constant moisture, at the same time avoiding too wet a condition. In the summer months that follow, careful attention should be paid to the watering; this is always an important subject with orchids, and even more so where seedlings are concerned.

At this stage the seedlings should be given as much heat as possible, approximately 60°F at night, rising to 80°F during the daytime. The humidity should be fairly high during the daytime, but if one is troubled by damping off in the early stages this may be controlled by lowering the humidity with less frequent damping down around the seedlings. By the time the winter has approached, with a summer's growth behind them, the seedlings should be strong and sturdy, and will not mind a night-time drop in the temperature to 55°F (13°C), with the appropriate reduction of the daytime temperature.

Fresh air is always important to seedlings, but without a draught, and here an electric fan can be of great value in keeping the air moving around the plants, especially during the winter months, when it is often impossible to open any ventilators. The seedlings should be fairly well shaded for the first few years of their life, and bright sun avoided at all times.

POTTING-ON

Seedlings in trays will probably remain undisturbed for twelve to eighteen months, whereas in community pots the seedlings may require potting on after only a few months if they have become too crowded. The best time to do this potting-on is about August, which will give the seedlings time to settle down again before the winter sets in. After August it is better not to disturb the seedlings until the following spring, when they have the summer growing season ahead of them again. The community-pot seedlings may require singling out, placing the plants individually into approximately 1½in pots, or by putting two or three to a pot, depending upon their size. The compost in the community pot having been finely chopped, it will be an easy matter to separate the roots without damaging them, and when potting-on the seedlings the method is the same as used for making up the community pot, but the wad of compost is split in half, and the seedlings sandwiched in between before firming the compost into the pot. By using this method there is no problem with long roots, and with a little practice one can soon learn to judge the size of the wad of compost needed to fit the pot.

When re-bedding the seedlings in peat and sand, it is better to trim back most of the roots, as it is impossible to get these back into the pot or tray without damage. These seedlings can either be re-bedded into a slightly deeper bed, or potted up singly in pots, but at this stage the compost should not suddenly be changed: it is better to keep the seedlings growing in the compost to which they have become accustomed.

One can expect to flower one's seedlings within five to six years, again depending upon the genera. This achievement can be crowned by registering one's own hybrid to the name of one's own choosing, provided, of course, this cross has not previously been made.

The authority for the international registration of orchid hybrids is the Royal Horticultural Society, from whom the registration form may be obtained. Should your cross have been previously raised, or your choice of name previously used, they will advise you accordingly.

MERISTEM CULTURE

We feel that meristem culture should be mentioned here, as many of the techniques for growing the young plants are the same as employed for raising seedlings.

Meristem culture is a method of mass-propagating a single clone (ie one individual plant) and producing many plantlets, which is also known as clonal multiplication. It was discovered as a direct result of research being carried out in France during the early 1960s on plants other than orchids, where a method of producing virus-free stocks from infected plants was being developed. It is now widely used to produce unlimited quantities of a particular clone.

In theory it should be possible to meristem all orchids, but in practice some will multiply more readily than others, while some genera have so far proved unsuccessful. Cymbidiums and Cattleyas are examples of easily meristemed orchids; Paphiopedilums, Phalaenopsis etc will not meristem. On the other hand, while Odontoglossums are very difficult, the multigeneric hybrids including Odontoglossum in their parentage, such as Vuylstekeara, reproduce quite readily.

The meristem is the nucleus of cells found in the centre of a growing tip of a plant. The meristem is cut out from a new growth when about $1\frac{1}{2}$in high under sterile conditions and is cultured in a flask where it grows first into a proto-corm, similar to the seedling, and finally into a plant. In its early stages of development this protocorm may be continu-ally divided at intervals. By this process any number of identical young plants may be produced over a period of months, while under normal methods of propagation it would take several years to build up a stock of even half a dozen flowering sized plants. But it must be remembered that these little plants will still require growing on for several years, and for this reason it is only worthwhile meristeming the very finest of orchids available.

When 2in high the young meristems resemble seedlings, except that they are stockier and more robust, and can be expected to reach flowering size at least twelve months before the seedlings.

From the point of view of the purchaser, it means he now has the choice either of buying an unflowered seedling on the basis of the quality of its parents, with the excitement of waiting to see what it will produce. Or he may purchase a meristem-grown young plant, in which case he is certain of the bloom that will result, which may well be a plant which has received an award. This is particularly useful for the per-son growing his orchids for cut flowers who may need large quantities of plants producing identical flowers at a certain time of the year.

Seven

Orchids for Exhibition

Once the amateur has become successful with the culture
and flowering of his or her plants, and can produce a well
grown plant in full bloom at the right time, he or she will
soon desire to show off this achievement, and rightly so. To
this end he may feel encouraged to exhibit his plants at
flower shows in the pursuit of a blue ribbon or two. There is
a tremendous growth of orchid societies up and down the
country, which nearly all hold exhibitions at various times
of the year, and these provide ample opportunities for exhibiting one's plants. Also, in some areas local horticultural
societies are being persuaded to include in their annual shows
special classes for orchid plants.

The way in which a plant is presented for display is most
important, and can sometimes tip the scales when it comes to
a 'photo finish' between two plants. Any orchid plant can be
suitable for exhibition; it does not necessarily have to be a
very expensive variety. Indeed, many of the less expensive
but showy species will often be placed above nondescript
hybrids. It should never be felt that one's own plants are
'not good enough', and you will probably be surprised and
delighted at your first results! The plant must, however, be a
healthy specimen, which has been grown to the best of one's
ability, and which is completely free from any pest or disease.
There is always someone to take delight in the discovery of a
mealy bug or scale insect hidden away in the new growth,

and apart from the embarrassment one would not wish to spread a pest onto the plants of the adjoining exhibit.

Preparing a plant for a show can start, as in the case of a Cymbidium, when the young buds have first left the sheath, and will require training in the right direction which is usually away from the foliage as much as possible, to show off the eventual blooms to their greatest advantage. The natural habit of the spike should not be interfered with; that is to say, if the Cymbidium is an arching or semi-arching variety, one should not attempt to tie it upright; only if it has a natural upright habit should it be tied in one or two places to an upright bamboo cane inserted into the compost, close to the bulbs and away from the pot rim where all the roots are. Cut it off a little below the topmost flowers, where less support is required. With the arching varieties a loose tie should be made just below the bottom or first bud, and as the spike develops it can be tied to a piece of strong wire; this should be bent to the same arch as the spike, with one end inserted into the top of a bamboo cane which has been cut off where the arch of the spike commences.

Where a Cymbidium has two or more flower-spikes on a plant, these can be encouraged to develop in different directions away from each other, again showing off the plant to best advantage. There is always a slight danger of big, heavy Cymbidium spikes snapping or bending over, and they should therefore be supported from an early age. Most of the Odontoglossums and Odontiodas will need only a short supporting cane with one tie just under the first bud; or again, if a very long spike, extra support can be given with an arching length of wire.

With Paphiopedilums, Cattleyas and their allies, if the plant is carrying more than one bloom, it is important that they should face the same way. A Paphiopedilum bloom should not be tied up until the flower has opened and become set, which usually takes a few days. Then a bamboo cane, preferably a green split cane for show purposes, can be inserted close to

Page 89:
(*right*) *Oncidium papilio;*
(*below*) *Vuylstekeara* Monica

Page 90: (*above*) *Cymbidium lowianum;* (*below*) *Cymbidium* Alexanderi 'Westonbirt' FC

the stem when held upright, and tied once immediately behind the flower, to make it 'look up'; if necessary a further tie is made lower down the stem. The cane is then cut off so as not to be seen above the dorsal petal. Now, if there are two or more flowers facing in different directions, it is easy enough to twist the cane and stem between thumb and forefinger until the required position is achieved. A thin piece of transparent sticky tape can be sometimes used around the stem behind the flower to prevent the flower from twisting back again.

Cattleya flowers can be moved around on their cane in the same way, but the method of supporting is slightly different. One cane should be used for each flower, each cane should have a split end and each must be just shorter than the top of the flower. Having correctly placed the cane, its split end can easily be opened with thumb and forefinger; at the same time the stem immediately behind the flower is placed in the split, which is then closed. The flower will be held firmly but gently, with no tying needed. By twisting the cane, the flowers are then arranged so that they do not touch each other, and the petals do not overlap. Apart from showing the blooms off better, this method will ensure that they do not damage each other, especially on their way to a show.

When travelling with long spikes, such as Cymbidiums, Odontoglossums or Phalaenopsis, etc, it is always a good idea to insert an extra cane in the compost at an angle, to which the end of the spike can be tied to keep it rigid during transit.

Many of the smaller-flowered species will require no extra support at all. Their own natural habits cannot be improved upon, unless they have a particularly long stem which may require support just for travelling, being removed for display. It is always best to remember that the less support visible on a plant, the better. Green bamboo canes are best, as thin as possible, with green string for tying.

The plant can now be smartened up by removing all old bracts from the leafless bulbs, stripping them downwards one

F

side at a time, and carefully from around the base of the newer bulbs with leaves. Any black leaf tips can be trimmed to a 'V', and any old foliage which has become spotted or badly marked is best removed or reduced, with any yellow foliage. The leaves can be polished simply by wiping them over with a clean dry sponge. With Cymbidium leaves, hold the base of each leaf with one finger and thumb for support, while the other holding the sponge runs along the length of the leaf. This will bring a good healthy-looking gloss to the plant—it is surprising how grubby the foliage can become over several months. Never attempt to clean the leaves of the new young growths in this way until their bulbs have matured; it is all too easy to pull out a leaf from the centre of the growth. The foliage of other plants can be polished in a similar way and at the same time a close check on insect pests should be made.

Where a flower is inadvertently damaged, perhaps receiving a broken petal or lip during transit, it can often be invisibly mended with the aid of a carefully placed thin strip of transparent sticky tape.

Where a plant is to be shown on its own as a single exhibit, a clean well-scrubbed pot can look as nice as anything, but where a group of plants is to be displayed, some form of covering for the pots and staging will add greatly to the general effect. In our opinion there is nothing more attractive than decorative moss, which gives a nice soft green base to the plants, and is more in keeping with their exotic dignity. This can be found growing in large sheets on trees and rocks in wet wooded valleys, but is also available from some orchid nurseries. It should always be used freshly gathered, and be well watered with liquid slug-killer before use. A suitably sized piece of moss is simply wrapped around the pot, tucked in at the top, and held in place with a rubber band or green string, which should not show, nor should there be any pot showing through the moss. When the group is completed, the staging and any stands that are used are also covered in moss.

Other methods can be used if decorative moss is not available. Spanish cork bark can be placed around the pots, with a carpet of crisp brown beech or oak leaves on the staging. Or you can have a black base by using black plastic pots with black velvet for the staging. In any case a piece of black velvet placed, where possible, behind the group of plants always does much to show off the blooms.

When you start arranging your plants, first mark the centre of your staging. Otherwise you may find upon completion that the plants are noticeably off centre. Now pick over the plants, grouping them into pairs, according to their size, height, colour etc; any plant which cannot be paired will be used for the centre. The best plants should also be reserved for the centre. Begin staging the group at the centre of the back row, arranging the plants, in their pairs, on each side, with the largest at the back and the smallest in the front, using stands where required; these can be covered-up pots or blocks of wood, etc. When completed, one side of your group should balance the other, with all the plants being as nearly as possible the same height on each side.

Some kinds of foliage plant can be used to support the display, but this should not be overdone; attention should be focused upon the orchids. This also applies where a class is based upon a theme; the theme should remain in the background, suggesting, or merely hinting, at the idea behind the display while the orchids remain to catch the eye.

Finally, it is important to see that each plant is correctly and clearly labelled with its name in full. Apart from finishing off a group of plants, this is also a rule at any RHS Show. But keep the label as small as possible; we find a green card is less distracting than white, attached to a thin wire stake which should be positioned just below the flowers. Adjustable wires can be purchased and are most useful. The plant's name should be written in full, either typed, or printed with a waterproof felt-tip pen.

One other point is worth mentioning: do be sure to read the

show schedule beforehand, and if you are not sure of anything, ask the show secretary. Check to see you have entered only species in the species class, and vice-versa; to have one's group disqualified upon a technical point is most disappointing.

When exhibiting at a two-day show in a very dry hall with central heating, it is advisable to give the orchids a good drink before leaving the greenhouse and, when the work of staging is completed, a good syringing of the staging. Moss will help to keep the plants from drying out completely, which is another reason in favour of using it. The moss can be sprayed as often as necessary, perhaps once a day, thus keeping your group looking green and fresh throughout the show.

Where the grower has flowered a plant which he considers to be of exceptionally outstanding quality and merit, this plant may be placed before the RHS Orchid Committee where it may be considered for either an Award of Merit or a First Class Certificate, or in the case of a well-grown plant a Cultural Commendation. However, the grower who has had no previous experience of this would be well advised to seek a professional opinion upon the quality of his plant first. Plants when submitted before the committee must be accompanied by a varietal name. If the plant receives an award the initials AM or FCC will be included after the name, for instance *Odontoglossum* Red Queen, 'Burnham' AM (plate p 18)—a distinction which only the one plant, or its propagations (including those from meristems) can hold.

Eight

Orchids for the Cut Flower

Orchids as a profitable hobby or commercial enterprise should also be mentioned. It would be a mistake for the owner of a modest collection to imagine that many hundreds of pounds profit can be made from his flowers without considerable outlay on greenhouses and suitably selected cut-flower stock. His flowers, however, can go a considerable way in helping with the fuel bill. Almost any long-lasting bloom is suitable for cut-flower trade, Cymbidiums, Odontoglossums, and Paphiopedilums being the most sought after. Cattleyas are sometimes required but by today's standards are mostly considered too large for floral work. Phalaenopsis are likely to flower at any time of the year but are more expensive to grow and provide a limited range of colours. The amateur may well enjoy his flowers for a week or two before parting with them, thus having enjoyment as well as some remuneration from them.

For the person who requires more from his orchids than a profitable hobby and wishes to grow them for the cut-flower trade as a source of income, Cymbidiums are undoubtedly the best genus to invest in. They can be grown in large beds on the ground by anyone who has little or no previous experience with orchids. No special greenhouse is required, but a house with glass sides down to the ground is most beneficial since it allows maximum light to reach the plants. The house should have ample headroom for the tall flower-spikes, and good ventilation. A reliable heating system should be installed where a minimum night temperature of 45/50°F can be maintained during the winter. Overhead spray rails, although not essential, are time-saving and advantageous to the plants during the summer months when they will keep up the humidity in the greenhouse. Plastic irrigation tubes laid between the plants will save time and labour on watering.

When preparing a new bed the amount of drainage required will depend upon the situation of the greenhouse and the water level in the ground. If the ground is made up of heavy clay for example, it may be necessary to raise the bed a foot or more from the ground, using a layer of coarse drainage such as brick rubble or clinker. Where the greenhouse is standing on naturally well-drained ground this sort of drainage in the bed may not be necessary.

An open, well-drained compost is used and made up of one part good quality peat, one part chopped bracken, one part leaf mould and a half part coarse sand, well mixed together. A liberal sprinkling of old cow dung (approx 8in pot to the sq yd) and hoof and horn meal (one handful to the sq yd) goes into the base of the bed, which is then made up to a depth of not less than 12in. The compost may differ slightly from the above depending upon the materials locally available, which should be taken advantage of, the proportions mentioned being used just as a guide. Between the drainage and the compost should be placed a layer of bracken which will prevent the compost from washing down into the drainage.

Before planting, the bed should be firmed down, well watered and allowed to settle for a couple of days. Where Cymbidiums previously pot-grown are to be planted out, all old compost should be removed from the roots, especially where the compost is a different type, such as moss and fibre. The roots should be trimmed back to a few inches. Seedlings, such as single growths or one pseudo-bulb and a growth, may be planted out a few inches to a foot apart, depending upon the space available and how long the plant is to remain in position. The seedlings should be firmly planted with the base of the plant level with the surface and not buried too deeply. Mature plants, whether they have been potted or are being rebedded, should be treated in the same way, trimming back the live roots and cutting out any dead ones.

After bedding, before the plants have settled down, a certain amount of leaf loss should be expected on the older pseudo-bulbs.

Provided the compost is kept in good heart with occasional topping-up, these plants will remain undisturbed for up to four or five years, depending upon the amount of growth made and in accordance with the amount of room allowed. When re-bedding is undertaken it will be found that Cymbidiums make long and extensive root systems just below the surface of the compost. It will be necessary to cut through these roots with a spade and lift the plant with a fork. The old compost is shaken off, all dead material removed and the live roots trimmed back to within a few inches. The plant can be divided if necessary and any back bulbs removed to be put on one side. After the bed has been cleared of all plants, it should be forked over, removing all remaining roots and dead leaves. The bed is then freshened up by adding new compost and built up again to its original height. The plants are rebedded at a distance of 2—3ft, staggering the rows to allow maximum space around each plant, leaving just sufficient room for a path down the centre of the greenhouse.

All planting and rebedding is best undertaken immediately after flowering in the spring. Plants bedded in the foregoing manner will make very rapid growth and greatly increase their size.

An alternative method to bed culture is to use stout wooden boxes approximately 2ft square. Although it may be necessary to give more individual attention to these plants than when in a bed, it is easier to be selective, removing any plant which may be suspected of having a virus disease, or whose flowers may be found to be below the standard required. Also there is the advantage of putting the plants out of doors during the summer where they can remain during the frost-free months of the year.

Once the initial hard work of preparing and planting the beds is completed, there is very little maintenance to be done until rebedding is again undertaken. In the spring it may be necessary to resurface the bed with a few inches of fresh compost as it settles.

The biggest difference between pot culture and growing Cymbidiums in beds is that once the plants are bedded out they will grow very much faster than in pots, and one can therefore allow the plants far more light than would otherwise be possible. For the first summer after bedding, when the plants are becoming established, it will be necessary to have some shading on the greenhouse. By the second year the plants will have made good root systems and should be growing strongly; they will be able to take full light with the ventilators wide open both day and night throughout the summer.

Cool nights are essential as an inducement to the flowering of these plants. They will require ample water at the roots and the beds should never be allowed to become dry at any time, otherwise a check in growth will result. Regular overhead spraying two or three times a day will greatly assist in keeping a good humid atmosphere.

With the approach of autumn and the appearance of the flower spikes overhead spraying should cease and the ventilators closed down at night, to be opened only on sunny days. Little or no ventilation should be needed during the winter when the beds should remain moist for longer periods, making watering more infrequent.

Spring is the busiest time, when the plants are flowering, and on very bright sunny days it may be necessary to protect the flowers from the sunlight, which can cause toning of the colours, especially in the pinks. A sheet of hessian or similar material may be tacked up on the inside of the glass as a temporary measure. An eye should be kept on any early bees which may be about, also any other predators. The overhead sprinklers should never be used while the plants are in bloom, but as soon as the last spikes have been cut, spraying may be recommenced.

Where plants are initially being purchased for the cut-flower trade, make sure they are perfectly healthy and free from any pests, which may spread rapidly through a bed. Those most sought by the florist are pinks, whites, greens and yellows in pastel shades, bearing in mind that most cut flowers are used for weddings or corsage work for evening wear. Medium-sized flowers are preferred to large ones, on short upright spikes of six to ten blooms.

To meet the needs of the market it is important to provide a steady flow of blooms throughout the season. Sending one box per week would be more satisfactory, and receive a better return, than to send three boxes in one week and no more for a month. Your buyer will come to expect a regular consignment and take orders in advance for his customers. Your Cymbidiums should therefore consist of early, middle and late flowering varieties.

There are so many suitable varieties available to chose from that a complete list would be impossible. We will therefore mention only a few famous parents, from which many of the finest modern strains suitable for the cut flower have been produced.

The Cymbidium season begins in November and December, at which time we can expect to have in flower the *C. tracyanum* and *C. erythrostylum* hybrids in a variety of colours. While perhaps lacking a little in quality there is always a great demand for these early-flowering varieties. In the new year they are followed by the early greens such as Nicky, a fine hybrid from Erica Sander, and the white and pink Coningsbyanum hybrids. During the spring hybrids from C. Alexanderi and Babylon will be flowering in various shades of pink, white and reddish-pink. Depending upon their breeding, these crosses should continue flowering until the end of the season.

The above mentioned Cymbidiums will produce the required short to medium spike which should require very little support while growing. Where a spike develops an arch it may be tied to an upright cane while it is still growing, making it easier for packing. The flower-spike may be cut at any time after the last flower has opened, or will last in perfect saleable condition for many weeks to suit the market requirements. The cut spikes can be put into a bucket of water overnight to give them a good drink before their journey to market if time permits.

The most suitable containers are Carnation boxes, lined with tissue paper, and six spikes can go to a box, or approximately fifty to sixty blooms. The spikes should be placed end to end and fixed with a cross bar to prevent movement. A little tissue paper may be tucked in between the blooms to prevent chafing or rubbing in transit. It is better not to pack too many flowers into one box; smaller boxes are more likely to realise a higher price per bloom than overcrowded ones.

Nine

The Most Popular Orchids

The orchids described in the following pages have been selected for their popularity among orchid growers. They consequently include some of the loveliest types, both species and hybrids, in cultivation today. They are not, however, listed in any order of popularity; for ease of reference they have been placed in their own sub-tribes, and these laid down in alphabetical order.

The orchid family is separated into tribes. These tribes are then divided into sub-tribes. Within the sub-tribes are the different genera, and these contain the individual species.

From time to time some orchids have been renamed by the botanists. Where this has occurred recently, and to avoid confusion to the reader, such plants have been placed under the name by which they are most commonly known. At the same time the name under which they are now classified is given in brackets.

When the species within one sub-tribe have been dealt with, we have followed this with a discussion on the most notable of the hybrids, giving an insight into the main breeding lines which had led up to the present-day varieties. This is concluded with remarks of any bigeneric of multigeneric hybrids which have appeared within the sub-tribe. This interbreeding of different genera is possible with very few other plants.

Where many thousands of hybrids have been made, only those of exceptional merit have been mentioned by name. Where no mention is made of hybrids within a particular sub-tribe, little or no hybridising of note has been carried out among the genera.

SUB-TRIBE BULBOPHYLLINAE

Bulbophyllum

The Bulbophyllums are hailed as being the largest genus of the orchid family, there being approximately two thousand species. They are closely related to the Cirrhopetalums with which they are now considered to be synonymous, and are therefore included under the one name in this book. It is to be expected that the distribution of such a huge genus is very wide, and indigenous species may be found in all the tropical and sub-tropical parts of the world, the greater concentration being in south-east Asia. Their native habitat may be on trees or rocks, where their creeping rhizomes are attached firmly by the strong wiry roots.

Basically the plants are bulbous and carry a single leaf per pseudo-bulb. There the similarity would appear to end; while one plant may consist of large pseudo-bulbs the size of a man's fist supporting a long leathery leaf, another may be so minute as to be overlooked at the first glance. The pseudo-bulbs may grow in tight clusters, or spread widely on long creeping rhizomes. Nearly all of them grow naturally in large tangled clumps, producing many aerial roots, which are usually thin and wiry.

The flower-spikes appear from the base of the pseudo-bulb, or sometimes from the half-completed growth, usually forming a cluster or rosette of blooms at the apex of the stem. This spike may be short, the flowers nestling among the bulbs, or stand tall and erect holding the blooms clear of the foliage. The spikes may be one to many flowered.

The size and shape of the flowers is so manifold that one cannot describe a typical form. They are noted for having moving parts and in several of the species the remarkable sepals are elongated and taper to a point, while the small petals are often tufted with tasselated hairs, which quiver in the slightest breeze. The lip is generally very small and inconspicuous; occasionally it may be fairly large and hinged lightly so that it will actually rock when alighted upon by a visiting insect. In other species the flowers resemble the open beak of a

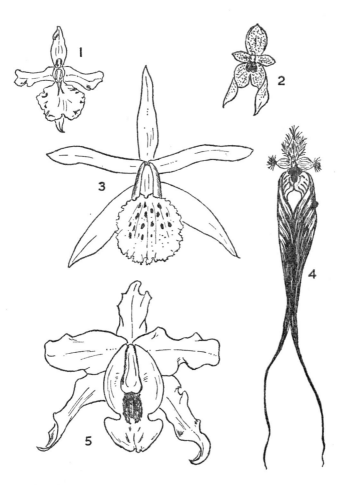

(1) *Rodreguezia venusta*   (2) *Bulbophyllum guttulatum*
(3) *Pleione formosanum*   (4) *Bulbophyllum collettii*
(5) *Coelogyne cristata*

bird. These flowers are often striped and spotted, and may differ in colour from pure white to almost black, with orange, red, yellow and brown being the most prominent colours. Quite a number of them are scented, while others possess unpleasant odours. By far the greater number of species are very small and mainly of botanical interest.

The plants may be accommodated in the cool, intermediate and hot houses, and being such a diverse group of plants, it is impossible to give a general outline of culture for them all, for a number have special individual requirements. Most of them dislike too much disturbance at the roots, and these are best accommodated in baskets or shallow pans using well-drained materials as used by other epiphytes, where they may be undisturbed and allowed to grow into large clumps, the rhizomes growing well beyond the rim of the pot. Their extensive root system will then become well established. They need a fairly light position at all times, and a decided rest during the winter.

B. barbigerum. A most interesting West African species whose flower spikes are about 7in long, the flowers being produced for about half their length, and numbering up to half a dozen. Sepals and petals are small, while the lip, which consists of a mass of short bristly hairs of a dark brown which are continually waving with the slightest movement of the air, gives a lifelike appearance to the flower. Being a plant of tropical origin it should be grown in the hot house. The flowering period is early summer.

B. collettii. This is a very attractive and free-flowering species. The flower-spike comes from the base of the half-completed new pseudo-bulb; it grows to 3 or 4in and carries up to six blooms. The dorsal sepal and petals are very small and bear tufts of moving hairs. The lip is small and inconspicuous. The sepals are held close together and are very broad at the base tapering to fine points about 6 inches long. The colour is a rich maroon, the base of the sepals striped with yellow. The species comes from Burma and will grow in the cool house (drawing, p 103).

B. dearei. Flowers borne singly, with large dorsal sepal, the petals and lateral sepals of equal proportions; the lip is curiously hinged and is capable of turning upside down. The flower is of a very pale yellow, various parts being spotted and striped maroon. It flowers in the summer and should be grown in the intermediate house. The species comes from the Philippines.

B. guttulatum. The flowers are carried side by side forming almost a complete circle on a 6 inch stem to give an umbrella-like shape. The individual flowers are small, up to an inch across, the lateral sepals curving inwards; the whole flower is a pale yellow evenly covered with delicate maroon dots; the lip is more heavily marked. This is a cool-house species from India which flowers at various times, often twice a year (drawing, p 103).

SUB-TRIBE CHYSINAE

Chysis

Only two species go to make up this genus of orchids. These are nevertheless handsome plants and their distribution covers a considerable area of tropical America, although these days they are more commonly obtained from Mexico. These epiphytic plants have long fleshy pseudo-bulbs, very thin at the base, which bear leaves of the same length. In nature the plant usually has a pendent habit. Several flowers are produced at a time, in a cluster from inside the leaves of the very young growth.

The plants are best grown in shallow pans or baskets, in a well-drained compost of moss and fibre, and hung in the intermediate house where a decided rest during the winter is necessary to produce flowers. While the plants need a sunny position, care should be taken not to overdo this to the extent of scorching the soft foliage.

C. bractescens. The beautiful flowers produced in spring, are of a waxy texture, large, rounded and very fragrant. The sepals are broader than the petals, both being a creamy white. The lip is small and yellow with a few red lines.

SUB-TRIBE COELOGYINAE

Coelogyne

This is a very widely distributed genus, the species being found from China to the Pacific Islands of the Fijis. Although this genus consists of well over a hundred known species, very few are in common cultivation. Those which are seem to be very popular. They are usually epiphytes, sometimes found growing on rocks. Coelogynes are bulbous orchids, these usually bearing a pair of broad leaves, the bulbs joined by a creeping rhizome. The leaves usually remain for some years.

The species mentioned produce their flower spikes from within the centre of the young growth, and flowering is usually completed before the pseudo-bulb has made up. The one exception to this however, is *C. cristata* whose flower spike is always produced from the base of the pseudo-bulb. The flowers are borne in sprays, which may be upright, arching or pendent. The flowers are neat, the segments being equal in size and the basic colour usually white, although green, yellow and buff-coloured species are mentioned. As the buds of these orchids develop they are covered in a protective sheath, which falls away upon blooming.

These are both cool and intermediate house subjects, and most of them need a decided rest if they are to flower properly, after the season's growth has been completed and the plant has become dormant. In the spring, when the plants are starting their growth and flowering, water may be gradually increased so that they are wet at all times. The new growth at this stage

age 107: (*above*) *Laeliocattleya* Miriam Marks: (*below*) *Paphiopedilum hirsutissimum*

Page 108:
(*above*)   *Dendrobium   brymerianum*;
(*right*) *Paphiopedilum argus*

is tube-like and will hold unwanted water only too easily. Care must be taken not to allow water to remain for too long in these new growths, which may cause damping off of the buds or spikes.

Repotting should only be undertaken when absolutely necessary, when the new growth is just beginning to show and certainly before the new root development commences. Many of the species are most suited to culture in shallow pans or on blocks of tree fern, in a compost consisting of moss and fibre, although for some species peat or loam may be added.

C. barbata. A species for the cool house. A robust plant with egg-shaped pseudo-bulbs which bear a pair of leaves approximately a foot long and 2in wide. The flower-spike is erect and may produce up to six flowers in succession. The petals are narrower than the sepals, and all are a pure crisp white. The lip is brown with a margin or fringe of dense hairs. The blooms are usually produced in the autumn or winter, and last well.

C. cristata. A great favourite for many years and very often recommended as a beginner's orchid owing to its endurance of great extremes in treatment, although not always flowering freely without correct treatment. The plants grow in tight clusters of round, shiny, light-green pseudo-bulbs resembling a bunch of grapes. The blooms are produced in late winter or spring in drooping sprays from the base. Prior to opening the buds have the appearance of being withered, when in fact they are quite healthy. Two to three flowers and sometimes more are produced, up to 4in across and of an intense crystallised white, except for a wide yellow streak in the throat. The edges of all the segments are crisped and waved. The flowers are long-lasting (drawing, p 103).

There are two distinct varieties which are *C. cristata* var *alba*, whose flowers are of the purest white without any trace of yellow, and *C. cristata* var *lemoniana* where the lip is marked with a citron-yellow stain. In these varieties the pseudo-bulbs

G

appear further along the rhizome than in the type. The plant is found over a wide area; most of the plants in cultivation come from the Himalayas, where they grow at high elevations.

This plant makes very little root and resents repotting unless absolutely necessary. Therefore it is best cultivated in large pans when a fresh compost containing some peat or loam may be tucked in between the pseudo-bulbs as necessary, where possible tucking in the creeping rhizome as the plant grows. In this way it may remain undisturbed in the same pan for many years. After the season's growth is completed it is essential, if flowers are to be produced, to give this plant a decided rest, even to the extent that the pseudo-bulbs shrivel considerably. This is not harmful: they will plump up again when the growing season is recommenced. *C. cristata* does well in a fairly light position in the cool house.

C. elata. A large growing species whose stout light-green pseudo-bulbs are 5 to 6in high, and 5 to 6in apart along a creeping rhizome. The stiff leaves are long and broad. The flower spike is seldom taller than the foliage, and carries five to ten blooms on an erect scape; these are 2 to 3in across, with sepals and petals of pure white. The lip is prettily marked with yellow and orange. Because of the long, thick woody rhizome this plant is more easily accommodated on a branch or long piece of bark on which it may be hung up in the cool house.

C. flaccida. An erect-growing species, with oblong pseudo-bulbs 2 to 3in high, growing close to each other. They are of a dark green, bearing foliage of the same colour, and becoming ribbed with age. The pendent sprays are produced in the spring when the growths are very young, bearing seven to ten flowers 1in or more across. They are a pale buff colour, the lip white with orange to yellow in the throat, and are long lasting and very fragrant. This plant must have a decided rest in the cool house with plenty of light to induce it to bloom.

C. massangeana. This is a large robust plant of typical habit. The pendent spikes can be up to 20in long, bearing many flowers about 2½in across, with sepals and petals of equal size of a pale yellow. The lip is prettily marked with brown and yellow veins. A good grower, intermediate house conditions suiting it best.

C. mooreana. A beautiful species whose pseudo-bulbs are borne close together, light green in colour and well rounded. The flower spike is erect carrying six to eight large drooping flowers. The blooms somewhat resemble those of *C. cristata,* with broad sepals and petals of a crisp white, while the lip is clearly marked with an intense golden-yellow. Like other Coelogynes this plant should be resting when not in growth, but with this species severe shrivelling should be avoided as it will take a long time to recover. The variety *C. mooreana* Brockhurst FCC is even more beautiful than the type.

C. ochracea. A very pretty and sweetly scented species from India. It is a neat grower, the whole plant not more than 8 to 10in high, and can be easily accommodated in a 3 or 4in pot. It will often produce several flowering growths at a time, making a most lovely display in the spring. The small flowers are white, the lip marked with irregular yellow blotches each bearing a margin of orange. This species will grow in a compost to which peat or loam is added. It is an easy-to-grow cool house plant which should have a place in every collection (plate, p 71).

C. pandurata. A very striking species in which the pseudo-bulbs are large, stout and compressed, produced well apart on a thick creeping rhizome. The two leaves are very large and broad, and the whole plant is a dark green colour. The flower scapes are produced in the spring, arching for about two feet, with up to a dozen 4in flowers, the sepals and petals of which are a clear bright green. The lip is narrow and long, somewhat resembling a violin in shape. The crest is warted and veined with black, giving the plant its affectionate name of the 'black orchid'. Found from Borneo to Malaya, it is best grown in long baskets in the intermediate to hot house.

Dendrochilum

Some handsome species are included in this genus, which is very often labelled as *Platyclinis,* but to be correct is now *Dendrochilum.* The species are to be found over a wide area of the East Indies, but most of the cultivated plants originate from the Philippines, where they may be found growing on rocks or low branches of trees at comparatively high elevations. The plants produce small oval pseudo-bulbs with a single leaf. The growth when young is heavily sheathed and produces its very thin and wiry flower spike in a graceful arch from the apex. The individual flowers are always small and insignificant, but on the dense spike produce a pleasing array of blooms arranged in two distinct rows, giving off a powerful perfume.

The culture of these plants is not difficult and most of them do best when grown in the cool house under shady conditions, never being allowed to become too dry at any time. Severe shrivelling of the bulbs should be avoided, although of course less water will be required during their short resting period. A basic compost of moss and fibre in equal parts to which loam or leaf mould or a little peat may be added, will suit them well. They may be grown in pans, and look their best when cultivated into large specimen plants.

D. cobbianum. The flowers are densely packed in two rows down each side of a long pendent spike. The colour is creamy white with an orange lip. It flowers in the spring.

D. filiforme. The flower spike of this very dainty species is extremely thin and hair-like. The small individual blooms are star-shaped and canary-yellow in colour. Well over a hundred contribute to make up the spike which spirals delicately downwards, giving a most charming effect: one can see why it is called the 'Golden Chain Orchid'. It is spring flowering.

D. glumaceum. Similar to *D. cobbianum,* but the flowers are usually less dense on the spike, the tips of the long petals turning upward. The flowers are a pale yellowish-white and strongly perfumed. Spring flowering.

Pleione

Pleiones were at one time classified with the *Coelogynes,* but are now kept separate. They are extremely popular, even among non-orchid growers; being of such easy culture they are grown alongside alpine plants. They are to be found growing at high altitudes, often on the snow-line in the Himalayas as far as China and across to the island of Formosa. The plants consist of squat round pseudo-bulbs of annual duration, each with a single leaf which is deciduous. In the spring, when the new growth develops, the flower spike is produced from the centre; it usually has one bloom which is 3 to 4in across and large for the size of the pseudo-bulb, and lasts a week to ten days. The sepals and petals are of equal proportions, usually of a delicate pink and the lip is large, frilled and spotted.

The plants should be repotted annually, either before or just after flowering, but certainly before new roots appear, into a rich compost of peat or loam, containing some dried cow manure and sand or grit. Any number of bulbs may be potted together to fill a large pan. During the summer months they should be given copious supplies of water, never being allowed to become dry. During this period a liquid feed is also beneficial. As the new pseudo-bulb builds up, the old one decays completely. An individual pseudo-bulb will very often produce two growths from the base, and also numerous terminal bulblets, which will quickly grow on to flowering size, increasing one's stock of these orchids rapidly.

When the season's growth has been completed, the foliage is discarded by the plant as activity ceases. All that is necessary during the winter is to keep the bulbs away from frost, with no attention at all.

P. formosanum (*P. bulbocodioides*). This is the most popular of all the Pleiones. Its pseudo-bulbs are dark green or purple, and the flowers are a soft delicate pink with a large frilly lip which is variable, but usually creamy-white with numerous brown spots and a yellow throat. It is easily propagated, and flowers in the spring (drawing, p 103).

P. humilis. The pseudo-bulbs are small and pear-shaped, dark green to purple. The flowers are smaller than in *P. formosanum*, with sepals and petals white, sometimes faintly spotted purple. The lip is white with reddish-brown markings. It blooms during the winter.

P. praecox. The pseudo-bulbs are squarish, with a depression around the apex, coloured dark green heavily spotted with purple-brown. The flowers are produced in the autumn or early winter and are a rich rosy-purple, the lip usually darker. This species grows more in the winter, and it is therefore advisable to keep it at a slightly higher temperature than the foregoing species.

Hybrids

In the sub-tribe *Coelogyninae*, disappointedly very little hybridising has been done, and barely a dozen hybrids in all from this large group exist, with no intergeneric breeding recorded. Probably the only hybrid of note is amongst the Coelogynes and, although produced as long ago as 1911, is still to be seen in cultivation and greatly sought after. This plant is

C. Burfordiense (*C. asperata* x *C. pandurata*). It is similar to
C. pandurata, but of a paler colour.

SUB-TRIBE COMPARETTUNAE

Rodreguezia

A comparatively small genus of epiphytic orchids from
Brazil and other parts of South America, where they inhabit
the tropical regions. The plants produce rather small, flattened
pseudo-bulbs, which produce several stiff dark-green leaves.
The short, arching flower-spikes are produced from the base,
flowering profusely. The sepals and petals are of equal proportions while the lip is large and the whole flower of a
crystalline texture.

They are plants which like their roots to be in the air, and
therefore do well when attached to pieces of wood and placed
in a shady position in the Cattleya house. Otherwise they may
be grown in small pans, where the compost of moss and fibre
should be kept sweet and fresh. Water should be given throughout the year, the plants resting only slightly during the winter.

R. secunda. A very pretty species with an arching spike up to
6in long, the flowers are arranged in two rows on top of the
spike, the whole colour being a rosy-pink. Summer flowering
or various.

R. venusta. A charming species with pendent spikes of highly
fragrant flowers, which are pure white, with a large spreading
lip stained with yellow (drawing, p 103).

SUB-TRIBE CYMBIDINAE

Cymbidium

Cymbidiums are without a doubt the most popular orchids
in cultivation today. They are also the best orchid for the complete beginner to start with. They are the most accommodating

of cool house orchids, withstanding a considerable amount of neglect, extremes in their temperature and general culture; in their turn rewarding the grower with long sprays of fine showy flowers in an abundance of different colours. They may be white, cream, or yellow to green, and pink, red and bronze, with every shade in between. The sepals and petals are of

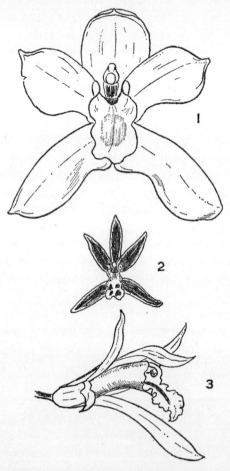

(1) *Cymbidium eburneum*   (2) *Cymbidium pumilum*
(3) *Cyperorchis mastersii*

equal size, and in a modern hybrid the wider the better, while
the lip is also broad and coloured with contrasting, usually red
markings, which may be spots, lines or a blotch. The flower-
spikes may be upright, arching, or pendent, with from half a
dozen blooms to maybe twenty or more, depending upon the
size of the plant and its breeding lines.

In a well-chosen collection the grower may have Cymbidiums in bloom for over six months of the year, the season
commencing in November/December, with the early pre-
Christmas varieties, to continue throughout the winter with
the mid-flowering types, and the later hybrids coming into their
own by March, April and even May.

The blooms will last for many weeks, although in fairness
to the plant it is always advisable to cut the flower spike after
the last flower has been open for about a week. The whole
spray may then be placed indoors in water, when it will last
just as long.

Cymbidiums grow into fairly large plants, making hard,
round, pseudo-bulbs bearing long strap-like leaves. The flower
spikes appear in the late summer, usually from the base of the
leading pseudo-bulb, which has developed during the summer.
Throughout the autumn and early winter the flower spike
slowly develops and when mature may be three or four feet
long. In the early stage the flower spike can be distinguished
from a new growth which may appear at the same time, by its
round plump shape. A new growth is always flatter and within
a short time divides into young leaves. As the flower spikes
develop and grow they will need attention in the form of a
supporting cane to which the spike can be tied just below the
buds.

During the summer Cymbidiums enjoy plenty of overhead
spraying several times a day, combined with plenty of water
at the roots. At this time of the year cool nights are essential
and a minimum temperature of 50°F (10°C) should be sought
after. If this is difficult to produce, the plants may well be
placed out of doors for the duration of the summer months,

provided they are placed in a shady position and kept free from slugs and other garden pests.

Repotting will be necessary when the leading pseudo-bulb has reached the rim of the pot, on average every other year with mature plants. The compost may consist basically of peat and sand, and the plant will often be returned to the same pot after the removal of a few of its back-bulbs. These back-bulbs will usually start to grow after being plunged in moss, thus increasing one's stock of a particular plant.

It is the hybrids which form the greater part of any collection today, these having taken over from the majority of species. However, there are still a few species which can and do hold their own among the modern hybrids, and are worthy of a place in the greenhouse.

The species are to be found from as far north as China to Australia in the south, from high up in the Himalayas to the coast-line of the China seas, from tropical rain-forests to dry rocky outcrops. It can be seen that Cymbidiums are very versatile and with their varying habitats have evolved into many different shapes and forms. But only a small handful of species from the Himalayas has been bred from, so that the modern hybrid of today bears no resemblance at all to some of the less familiar species. It is only the cool-growing types that have been bred from, and not the tropical or warm growing varieties which come from the East Indies.

In the early days it was always the plant with the largest flower and best shape that was looked to as a parent. Today, in comparison with the large, round and perfectly shaped blooms of the hybrids, the novelty of a small dainty plant draws the attention particularly for the amateur with only a small greenhouse, And so it is we find ourselves starting to breed on new lines from some of the lesser known and smaller species of the Cymbidium family which hitherto have been regarded as unimportant.

By crossing the miniature species with the modern hybrids we are seeing some truly beautiful flowers in the second and third generation, where the results in new shapes and colours are proving to be most rewarding.

C. canaliculatum. A specie from Australia which does best either in the warm end of the cool house, or the intermediate house. When the growth is completed it should be given a decided rest with plenty of light. The flowers are miniature and borne densely on the spike. Their colour is variable from olive-green to brown and in some varieties a blackish-purple. It has been found in the wild, growing 15ft up on a dead tree, where the roots have penetrated down through the inside of the trunk to the ground.

C. devonianum. A cool-house miniature from the Himalayas which is in great demand today as well as being a most promising parent for breeding miniature hybrids. The plant makes only small pseudo-bulbs with two to three broad, dark-green leaves.

The flower-spike appears in the late autumn to be in bloom from March to May. It is completely pendent—to the extent that if one is not careful it may bury itself in the compost. This is easily prevented by placing a small piece of label material just under the spike when in its early stages to guide it over the edge of the pot. The spike will grow approximately 12in long and produce a raceme of closely packed flowers, the basic colour of which is olive-green overlaid with lines of purple; the lip is marked with diffused purple blotches. This plant, once considered to be rare, is now happily very common (plate, p 71).

C. eburneum. This species has a long narrow pseudo-bulb and is usually heavily sheathed in foliage, the leaves being long and narrow, typical of the Cymbidium. The 3in flowers are produced late in the season on an upright spike, seldom more than two together. They are pure white with a yellow throat and quite fragrant. It is found growing at a fairly high elevation and is therefore suitable for the cool greenhouse (drawing, p 116).

C. erythrostylum. A very fine early-flowering species which has helped to produce many of the pre-Christmas pinks. Although the spikes are short several may be produced from a sizeable plant, with five to six flowers to a spray, their main characteristic being that the two lateral petals point upwards, a character which is carried forward into its hybrids. The flowers are white, sometimes slightly peppered with purple dots on the basal half of the petals. The lip is creamy-white marked with purple. This Indian species is suitable for the cool house. Although scarce today, many of its fine hybrids are available.

C. finlaysonianum. This is one of the Cymbidiums which are best grown in the intermediate house. Its leaves are similar in appearance to the type, but of a very much thicker texture. This species is to be found growing wild over an enormous range from as far north as Burma, Vietnam, the Malayan Peninsula and the Philippines down to Java and Borneo, usually growing on trees in sunny positions, where its long pendent spikes bear many flowers. Their colour varies according to the country, from yellow with a streak of red to a tawny-brown with the lip usually similarly marked, and blotched with a deep wine-red. These different colour forms from different parts of the world were at one time considered to be distinct species, such as *C. aloifolium, C. pendulum* and *C. tricolor,* but now are generally considered to be synonymous. Surprisingly little hybridisation has been done with this plant, although it may prove worthwhile in producing hybrids to grow in hotter parts of the world.

C. insigne. Although this species is almost unobtainable now, it is included here as it was at one time more common and was considerably used as a parent, nearly all modern hybrids claiming descent from this orchid. The plant is of typical structure; the erect spikes which carry a dozen or more flowers can be up to 4ft tall. The flowers are 3 to 4in across varying in colour from rosy-pink to almost white, and the bases of the petals and sepals are heavily marked with red. The lip is broad, usually darker with bright crimson markings. It is a very fine species, and it is a pity it is so scarce today.

C. lowianum. One of the most popular species in cultivation, this holds its place well among the modern hybrids. It makes a large, robust plant and is capable of producing long arching spikes of twenty-five or more flowers up to 4in across. The sepals and petals are green more or less suffused with brown, while the lip is cream blotched with red. This plant originates from Burma, whence it was introduced in 1878, and does well in the cool house, flowering during April and May. The variety *concolor* differs from the type by having greenish-yellow petals and the lip is blotched with yellow (plate, p 90).

C. pumilum. A dwarf-growing species from Japan with narrow leaves and carrying short erect flower-spikes of small flowers, reddish-brown with a yellow margin to the petals. The lip is white dotted and marked with similar reddish-brown. This is a very pretty plant suitable for the cool house. There are several named varieties of *pumilum,* of which *album* is a very pale form, while the variety *formosum* is a dark brick-red (drawing, p 116).

C. tigrinum. A dwarf-growing plant with pseudo-bulbs like walnuts, bearing two to three broad leaves. Up to three large flowers are borne on a short spike. The petals are narrow, pale greeny-yellow with dotted lines of crimson. The hairy lip is creamy-white and is also spotted and striped. To flower this plant successfully it is necessary to give maximum light and a complete rest after the season's growth is completed, to the extent that the pseudo-bulbs shrivel considerably. This will induce the embryo flower-spike into activity. When this is seen watering may be recommenced prior to the flowers opening in the spring. This plant is a native of Burma where it frequently grows on exposed rocky outcrops.

C. tracyanum. A strong, robust-growing Cymbidium making large bulbs with plenty of foliage, typical of the type. When not in flower it can be recognised by the small upright roots on the surface of the compost, appearing like miniature stalagmites. The flower-spikes, which are at their best in the autumn, are long and semi-arching with 10 to 15 large flowers, the narrow petals and sepals are beige-yellow, usually with broken lines of crimson. The lip is hairy, creamy-yellow and spotted with reddish-brown. It is certainly the most strongly fragrant of the Cymbidiums and well worth a place in the cool house.

Cyperorchis

This is a small genus from Burma very closely related to Cymbidium, and often included with that genus. The plants are, however, identifiable by their bell-shaped flowers and slightly differing habit. They will hybridise quite readily with Cymbidiums, when the progeny are classed as Cymbidiums. The culture, compost and general requirements are the same as for Cymbidiums.

C. elegans. A moderate sized plant of typical Cymbidium habit. The spikes are produced in the autumn and grow and develop quickly into an arching raceme of many, closely set pendent flowers of a pale straw-yellow. Slightly fragrant.

C. mastersii. The plant has a tendency to be continually growing from the centre rather than having several pseudo-bulbs. The flower-spikes, usually two or three at a time, appear from the axils of the leaves and carry three to four flowers which are ivory-white with a yellow throat and very fragrant (drawing, p 116).

Hybrids

Cymbidium hybrids are far too numerous for many specific names to be mentioned here. Instead we will merely introduce the reader to a few of the better known plants which have proved themselves over the years to be fine parents, and are responsible for producing the hybrid of today.

Of all the orchids used for breeding no name crops up so regularly as that of the famous *Cymbidium* Alexanderi 'Westonbirt' FCC. This plant has been responsible for producing more hybrids of exceptionally fine quality than any other parent (plate, p 90). The interbreeding of three species, namely *C. lowianum, C. eburneum* and *C. insigne* produced *C.* Alexanderi, giving a solid round flower with pure white, heavily textured flowers, four to seven on a spike, with spotted red lips. Although this plant was first registered as long ago as 1911, it is still being used to breed from. Among its best-known progeny is Rosanna 'Pinkie' FCC (*C.* Alexanderi 'Westonbirt' FCC x Kittiwake 1927) famous in its own right as a parent. This plant has brought a delicate shade of pink into the very round petals, while the lip is slightly blushed with pink (plate, p 53). Balkis is the result of crossing *C.* Alexanderi 'Westonbirt' and Rosanna 'Pinkie', registered in 1934. There are many fine named varieties of Balkis available, which are among some of the best whites. And so we see that *C.* Alexanderi is still very important in producing good shapes and heavily textured flowers.

The long arching spikes of pink flowers are generally regarded to have begun with *Cymbidium* Pauwelsii 'Compte de Hemptine' FCC 1911. This was the result of crossing *C. insigne* with *C. lowianum,* combining the pink colour of *C. insigne* with the long arching habit of *C. lowianum.* Numerous hybrids have been raised from this plant and when crossed with

Olympus (*C.* Alexanderi 'Westonbirt' x Vesta) produced Babylon 'Castle Hill' FCC, which gave us the large, round, open
and beautifully marked lips. From Babylon came Vieux Rose
(Babylon 'Castle Hill' x Rio Rita 'Radiant') one of the most
notable hybrids in this line, which, in turn, crossed with *C.*
Alexanderi 'Westonbirt', gives Western Rose, registered in
1965, which has produced beautiful soft pinks.

Two green species are responsible for commencing the lines
of green hybrids. From *C. lowianum* come the very fine
blotched-lip hybrids such as Pearlbel and Miretta, of which
there are many fine awarded varieties, and their hybrids
Centurion, Loch Lomond var Mem J. B. Russon AM 1968.
From *C. grandiflorum* come the more softly textured flowers
with usually cream lips, delicately spotted. A few examples
of the best parents are Erica Sander, Nicky and Irish Mist, the
latter two being crossed to produce Larne (plate, p 35).

Red is a colour not represented in the species; this has been
produced by selective breeding through the pink lines. The
first red of any merit was Flare, which made its appearance in
1946, the most notable being the red Flare 'Dell Park' FCC
in 1954. One of the nicest plants raised from Flare is Magna
Carta, produced by crossing with Runnymede, the latter being
produced from Babylon 'Castle Hill' and Roxana.

The above lines of hybridising have been continually striv-
ing to improve the shape and the colour and particularly the
size, each generation becoming larger than the last. Inevitably,
a demand has arisen for smaller plants with smaller flowers,
and here the miniature species have played the greatest part.
C. pumilum when crossed with *C. insigne* produced Minuet,
which received an Award of Merit in 1949 and really stirred
a new interest in the small, free-flowering hybrids. It was not
long before many fine seedlings started to appear although
second generation hybrids seemed difficult to produce at
first. When *C. pumilum* was crossed with *C.* Alexanderi it
produced Sweetheart, which when crossed back with *C.* Alexanderi produced the very succesful Showgirl, which improved

Page 125:
(*left*) *Paphiopedilum* Clair de
Lune 'Egard van Belle' AM;
a fine Maudiae hybrid;
(*below*) *Phalaenopsis* Zada

Page 126:
(*left*) a mature Cymbidium seed po[...]
(*below*) A flask and community pot [...]
Cymbidium seedlings

the shape and texture of Sweetheart. These two had pastel colours. By crossing *C. pumilum* with Babylon, the darker pink Oriental Legend appeared. Crossed with *C. lowianum*, *C. pumilum* produced the golden-yellow Pumilow (plate, p 35), but although pretty in colour, this hybrid lacks good shape. More hybrids have been raised from *C. pumilum* than any other miniature species and by using the different colour variations differently coloured hybrids have been obtained.

The second most popular miniature species to be used for breeding is *C. devonianum*. This flower, totally different from *C. pumilum,* has given us the dark rich colours to be found notably in Touchstone 'Mahogany' AM 1967. This is a perfectly rounded flower of a rich mahogany and a large heavily blotched lip, which is typical of seedlings produced from *C. devonianum*. When *C. devonianum* is crossed with *C. pumilum,* the result is the very charming Miss Muffet. *C. devonianum* was first used as a parent as long ago as 1911 when it was crossed with *C. lowianum* to produce *C.* Langleyense. Although little interest at the time was paid to them, now that miniatures are in vogue, some of these old crosses such as Volesang, have been remade, and have been received with great interest. The modern cross of *C. devonianum* with Nicky gives Goblin with perfectly shaped little olive-green flowers, with a delicately marked lip (plate, p 35). There is no doubt that the future of *C. devonianum* is bright, and the best hybrids have yet to be raised.

There are a number of other species which will give miniature or semi-miniature hybrids, but at present have only been used to make a few novelty crosses such as *C.* Alexanderi x *C. finlaysonianum*, producing Alpine Rose, and *C.* Alexanderi x *tigrinum* to give Tiger Tail. Several hybrids have been raised from *C. ensiflorum,* a straw-yellow miniature, of which Peter Pan (*C. ensiflorum* x Miretta) is one example.

H

SUB-TRIBE CYPRIPEDILINAE

Originally plants in this sub-tribe were known collectively as Cypripediums, until they were divided into four groups, these being *Cypripedium, Paphiopedilum, Phragmipedium* and *Selenipedium.*

These constitute one of the oldest groups of orchids in existence. Their flower structure and particularly the stamens are unique, being found nowhere else in the orchid kingdom. The distribution of these plants is very wide and they are spread over a large area of the globe.

Cypripedium

The true Cypripediums are a very widely distributed genus and are to be found growing wild in the temperate zones of the continents of the northern hemisphere like our almost extinct Lady's Slipper Orchid, *C. calceolus,* still fairly common in Europe. They are usually cultivated along with alpine plants or in a woodland garden, and are not so often seen in the orchid house, and will therefore not be more fully discussed.

Paphiopedilum

Paphiopedilums, numbering approximately fifty known species, extend from China across the Himalayas into India and throughout south-east Asia to New Guinea. It is this group of plants that were formerly known as Cypripediums, by which name they are still often referred to; they are usually offered for sale as Cypripediums, and even tabulated in the hybrid list as such. This technically incorrect labelling is likely to persist, as one may sometimes prefer to use the name by which a plant has been traditionally known. For the purpose of this book we have chosen to list the species under their correct names.

In the wild they are usually terrestrial but sometimes grow

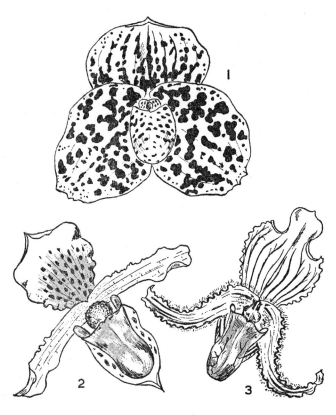

(1) *Paphiopedilum bellatulum*   (2) *Paphiopedilum insigne*
(3) *Paphiopedilum fairrieanum*

on rocks or occasionally as epiphytes. The plants are bulbless, producing growths of thick fleshy leaves, these being their only reservoir of moisture; the flower-spike emerges from the centre of the growth, on which may be one to three and in some species more flowers. The foliage may be of a solid green or a beautiful mottled pattern of light and dark green which makes these orchids extremely attractive plants. Most of them are of compact size, seldom requiring anything larger than a 4 or 5 inch pot, taking up little room on the staging.

The blooms, which are held upright on the stem, or are sometimes drooping, differ from other orchids in their extraordinarily developed segments. The top sepal is in most species developed into a large, round and very showy canopy which is referred to as the dorsal sepal. The bottom two sepals are usually insignificant. The labellum or lip is formed into a slipper-shaped pouch, hence the name 'Lady's Slipper Orchid' also given to this group. The lateral petals are usually large and colourful and in some species extremely elongated. The whole impression is one of a waxy texture, often shining as if varnished. The main attractions of the Paphiopedilums are the longevity of their blooms which will often last for many months in perfection, and the amazing abundance of colour and design to be found in the petals which are often lined or covered with hairs and warts.

Being bulbless, these plants should never be allowed to become dry for long periods. They have no definite resting period and should be grown in shady and well-ventilated greenhouses in the cool or intermediate sections. Generally speaking, the plain or green leaved varieties are cooler growing than those with the mottled foliage.

Their shading should be heavy, especially in the summer, and strong direct sunlight should never be allowed to play on the foliage. Conditions similar to those for Odontoglossums will often suit them.

A well-drained compost of equal parts of moss and fibre is the most suitable for the hybrids, although a number of the species will flourish in a compost with one-third of fibrous loam added. The plants can be propagated readily by carefully removing the back growth as one would remove a back bulb. It is advisable to cut the rhizome a few months before the plant is repotted, by which time the severed portion will have started to grow and established itself as a separate plant. One should not, however, rush into doing this too often, for a large specimen plant with several growths will produce stronger and larger flowers, as well as giving a more pleasing display.

One should avoid the temptation to chop the plant into single growths, thus ending up with small pieces that will not flower for some time.

On the subject of pests, these plants seem to keep themselves remarkably free of red spider and scale, which readily attack other orchids. The greatest danger lies in overwatering the plants, or allowing water to lie in the top of the growths overnight, during periods of low temperature, when decay will quickly set in, resulting in the loss of the growth and possibly the plant.

P. argus. A striking species originating from the Philippines which should be grown in the intermediate house and kept well shaded. The foliage is slightly mottled and the plant will flower freely, even off a single growth. It produces a very long stem which may be up to 18in tall, carrying a single flower the colour of which is liable to vary considerably. Basically it is green, the dorsal sepal lightly or heavily striped in purple; the pouch is a dull purple, and the petals striped and spotted with several hairy warts along the top edge. It will last for many weeks in perfect condition. Flowering period May and June (plate, p 108).

P. bellatulum. A much sought-after orchid which is very scarce today. It is a dwarf plant from Thailand. The squat foliage is mottled a blue-green and covered in a glorious sheen. The undersides of the leaves are often a rich purple. These leaves are extremely brittle and great care should be exercised when handling or potting. The flower stem is never more than a few inches long and may bear one, or rarely two, flowers. These are approximately 3in in diameter; the dorsal sepal and the two petals are very large and rounded, giving the flower a cupped appearance. The pouch is small and egg-shaped, the whole flower being white, spotted and flushed with reddish-purple. There also exist a few, very rare, albino forms. This plant is best grown in the intermediate house where it will bloom late in the winter, or in early spring (drawing, p 129).

P. callosum. An extremely handsome and common species
from Thailand. The wide leaves are mottled pale green. This
is a good and easy grower, which will often produce several
growths at a time. The tall flower-stem bears a single flower 4in
or more across. The large dominant dorsal sepal is green at the
base and heavily lined with purple on a white ground. The
slender petals are similarly marked and bear several large
black warts on the top edge. The narrow pouch is pale green
sometimes tinted purple. It is one of the coolest growing of the
mottled varieties and can therefore be accommodated in the
warmest end of the cool house, or in the intermediate house.
Flowering time spring.

P. concolor. This species is similar in habit and cultural requirements to *P. bellatulum*. The leaves are paler in colour,
while the flowers are smaller The basic colour of the flower
is a creamy-yellow, with a fine peppering of dark colour.

P. fairrieanum. A delightful species for the cool house, which
hails from the Himalayas. The foliage is short and of a pale
green. The slender flower-stems carry a single small flower
which is basically green and white. The large dorsal sepal has
an extremely wavy edge with purple veins running from the
base and becoming branched at the edges. The petals are
drooping, the ends curling upwards, outlined with a heavy
purple edging, and fringed with small hairs. The pouch is
narrow, of a light greeny-brown. Autumn-flowering (drawing,
p 129).

P. hirsutissimum. With long strap-like leaves of a heavy dark-
green colour, this is a most robust grower, suitable for the
cool house. The flowers are produced on a hairy stem up to
10in tall. The dorsal sepal is comparatively small, pale-green,
very heavily peppered with brownish-purple. The very long

petals, which are held straight out from the flower, are club-shaped and the edges are extremely wavy, the basal half being peppered and spotted with brown while the end portions are of a pastel pink. The pouch is brown and green. This handsome species flowers freely in the spring (plate, p 107).

P. insigne. Easily the best-known of all orchids, and a very old favourite. These plants may often be found in conservatories where they have been grown for many years into huge clumps, apparently thriving with very little attention and blooming freely. One can often be shown such splendid specimens which have not been repotted for twenty years! This orchid has been cultivated since the earliest days of greenhouses, and in the Victorian era there were several dozen named varieties. Unfortunately, few of these are available now.

The plant consists of plain green leaves and the flower scapes are 6 to 9in tall with a single flower produced at Christmas time. The dorsal sepal is green with brown spots and a broad white margin. The petals are brown with a margin and tip of green. The pouch is similarly coloured and very shiny. The most outstanding variety is 'Harefield Hall', where the blooms are much larger and the dorsal sepal more rounded. Another noteworthy variety is *P. insigne* var *sanderae*, in which the bloom is a greeny-yellow, the dorsal sepal green and margined white, the whole flower devoid of the brown markings found in the type. These will grow in almost any compost, and are very often potted in pure loam and grown in the cool end of the cool house (drawing, p 129).

P. niveum. The foliage of this species is similar to *P. bellatulum*, the surface being of a marbled blue-green and the underside of purple. The leaves are usually a little narrower and shorter than in *P. bellatulum*. The stem is 4 to 5in tall and carries the one or very occasionally two flowers clear of the foliage. The small roundish flowers have a broad dorsal sepal and petals, with a spheroid pouch. The whole flower is a pure crisp white with a fine peppering of pink near the centre of the bloom. It should be potted in a well-drained compost and grown in the intermediate house, or hotter.

P. philippinense. A slow-growing plant with hard, plain green foliage which makes large robust growths. The 10in flower-spikes carry three or four blooms. The small white dorsal sepal has a few uneven dark veins, the pouch is ochre yellow with faint brown lines and the petals, which are amongst the longest of the Paphiopedilums, hang down to a length of 5 or 6in, narrow, ribbon-like and twisted throughout their length. The base is green but soon turns to a rich purple for the remaining length. This plant comes from the Philippines and should be grown in the intermediate to hot house. Flowering period late spring.

P. spicerianum. An attractive species with dark-green leaves, the growths heavily spotted at the base. The large, pure-white dorsal sepal predominates; this has a broad purple streak running from the centre to the tip, while the sides curl backwards. The narrow, pale green petals have wavy edges with a dark line down the centre, while the pouch is greeny-brown.

The plant may be accommodated in the cool house where it will grow alongside *P. insigne.* Autumn flowering and very long lasting.

P. sukhakulii. A species of fairly recent introduction from Thailand, with mottled foliage very similar to *P. callosum* and almost indistinguishable when not in flower. The small white dorsal sepal is heavily lined with dark green. The long flat smooth-edged petals are held out straight and vary considerably in their colouring, but are usually pale green densely or lightly spotted with brown-purple. The pouch is a pale reddish-green. Suitable for the intermediate house, where its flowers are produced in the late summer or autumn.

P. venustum. This species must surely have the most beautiful foliage of all, the leaves being tessellated in deep-blue and grey-green, while the undersides are flecked in purple and in some plants completely and evenly coloured. The flowers are modest, particularly for the size of the plant; the dorsal sepal is small, white, and heavily lined with green, the petals are lined with green at the base, turning dark pink at the tips, and covered in numerous warts and hairs. The orangey-yellow pouch is covered in heavy green veins.

Phragmipedium

A small genus, more commonly known as *Selenipedium,* but now correctly called *Phragmipedium.* The true *Selenipedium* is an even smaller genus, not in cultivation today. Although very striking and distinct, the Phragmipediums may be termed the forgotten orchids. Out of a dozen or so species once known, very few are seen today, and it is only very occasionally that one may come across an old primary hybrid, and these are so little known that they are usually considered to be species. It is to be regretted that at this present time no hybrids are made, and most of the hybrids in existence were registered a hundred years or so ago. At the turn of the century some fifty-odd hybrids were listed, of which only a few have survived in well-looked-after orchid establishments where, due to the care and attention given them, together with the fact that they are most robust growers, they have stood the test of time.

The species are all from tropical America where they are to be found growing as terrestrials or sometimes on rocks. For this reason they are best grown with the warm house Paphiopedilums where their culture is the same; although, since they make larger plants with taller scapes, they will need a little more room.

They all produce long strap-like pale to dark green foliage, with tall scapes and three to four flowers or more depend-

ing upon the species. In some species the flowers open in
succession. The predominant colours are greeny-buff to pink.
The pouch is often large and the dorsal sepal narrow, pointed
and drooping. The lateral petals can be very narrow and
ribbon-like, and attain a length of up to 30in. It is fascinating
to watch these flowers open: the petals are of the same length
as the other portions of the bloom, and quickly start to grow,
an inch a day, spiralling downwards until they attain their full
length.

Among the species the most noteworthy are perhaps *P.
caudatum* and *P. longifolium,* remembered for having produced several good hybrids. The best of these is P. Grande,
which can still be obtained today, and its variety 'Macro-
chilum', which is easily the most robust and the best to grow,
producing the most beautiful blooms. This plant was first recorded in 1881 when it was considered to be of exceptional
merit, and indeed, this is still true today.

Hybrids

From the very start of hybridising Paphiopedilums were
well to the fore, and breeders were successful in crossing and
raising new hybrids, until they became one of the most
popular genera of that time.

The breeders had the choice of the best of the species,
among them *P. insigne* and *P. spicerianum,* of which there
were at that time many excellent named varieties, to be used
for selective breeding. All the plain-leaved Paphiopedilums
today have these two plants somewhere in their pedigree.

In 1869 the first hybrid was produced, this being P. Harrisianum, the progeny of *P. villosum* and *P. barbatum.* This was
a great milestone and in fact P. Harrisianum and several of
its named varieties are still obtainable. It was very quickly
realised that these plants would readily interbreed and that
their seedlings would flower within a few years, quicker than
many other orchids. Amongst the early surprises were sup-

posedly new hybrids which when flowered turned out to be already known species. This proved that the plants collected from the wild were in fact natural hybrids, and not species as originally thought.

By the turn of the century, well over 1,000 hybrids were listed in the register, and this genus is still as popular now as it was then. New exciting hybrids are still being produced in a multitude of colours.

Among the plain-leaved Paphiopedilum hybrids, one of the most important parents has been Cardinal Mercier, which has been used extensively for breeding and in producing the more colourful blooms. This line has produced Paeony 'Regency' AM combining both shape and colour.

In the background of all the good yellows is to be found Diana Broughton, while F. C. Puddle is in the make-up of the lovely white-flowered Paphiopedilums such as Dusty Miller and Meadowsweet.

At one time the mottled-leaved Paphiopedilums were bred from considerably, but now there is less interest in these, although many of the beautiful and quite rare plants were hybridised from them. During this era one of the finest plants to be produced was P. Maudiae and many of its named varieties and subsequent hybrids, which are still available. The Maudiae type is well known to all orchid lovers for the ease with which it grows and propagates; its long stem and large, elegant white and green striped flowers will last for months in perfection.

SUB-TRIBE DENDROBINAE

Dendrobiums

This genus is considered to be the second largest of the orchids, consisting of approximately 1,600 distinct known species, and doubtless there are still a few to be discovered in the deep jungles of south-east Asia. Its distribution is enormous, from as far north as Japan and Korea right across parts of China to India, down through the Malayan Peninsula and Indonesia to New Guinea and the northern coast of Australia.

These orchids sometimes grow on rocks but are more usually epiphytic, growing in the dense jungles where they festoon the branches and trunks of their hosts, making a brilliant display of colour and filling the air with their strong fragrance when in bloom. Others may be found on the most exposed parts of mountainous regions growing on scrubby trees or rocky outcrops, where their growth is usually harder, adapting to their surrounding. All are noted for the daintiness of their numerous blooms, with their pastel shades and delicate texture.

It is only natural to expect from a group of such wide distribution that the variation in habit and floral structure, and also the cultural requirements, are considerable. Therefore to give a general description of these plants is not easy. However, basically the structure of the plant is a creeping rhizome which produces pseudo-bulbs which may be anything from an inch or two high to 4ft—so elongated and thin that they are usually referred to as canes rather than bulbs, and in the wild develop a drooping habit. These pseudo-bulbs may be deciduous at certain times of the year, or evergreen. The leaves can be produced along the whole length of the pseudo-bulb or with just a pair at the apex. The blooms may also be produced along the full length of the pseudo-bulb from the axils of the leaves, singly or in small panicles, or may appear in sprays from the apex.

The lip is usually the most attractive part of the flower, being often deeply blotched with a rich colour. The sepals and petals are usually equal in size.

It is not difficult to find Dendrobiums which can be grown in either the cool, intermediate or hot house. In the spring, when the new growths start to appear on the cool-house varieties, watering may be commenced and every effort made to encourage the new growth by giving as much water as the plant will take (but not overwatering), together with fairly heavy shade and plenty of warmth. During the summer months, by which time ample new roots will have been made, the plants may be kept wet and constantly sprayed, as many of them have to complete a stem of considerable length in a very short time.

In the autumn or early winter, when the terminal leaf appears and the season's growth is completed, the plants will begin their rest, and will take a lower night temperature, combined with more light and less water. This will induce the leaves to fall and the pseudo-bulbs to ripen prior to the development of the flower buds. In certain species, if the rest has not been adequately carried out, small plantlets will grow instead of flower-buds. It is therefore important that during this period of dormant growth watering should be greatly reduced or withheld altogether, even though the bulbs may shrivel slightly, and not recommence until the flower-buds or new basal growth start to develop. Full light is also essential at this time.

Where a cool and an intermediate house are available many of the Dendrobiums will benefit from being placed in the intermediate house, with its extra warmth and humidity, during the summer, and removed to the coolest and sunniest part of the cool house for the winter; of course others, though requiring the extra light, are best kept in the intermediate temperature at all times.

These extremes in culture are brought about by the fact that in nature they are subjected to long periods of drought followed by equally long periods of continuous rain.

The compost for these plants should of course consist of well-drained materials. Equal parts of moss and fibre will form a good basis. Compared with the size of the plant, most Dendrobiums do not make an extensive root system and therefore it is a mistake to overpot them, and the smallest pot possible should be found to accommodate them. Many of the dwarf-growing types will do well in pans or half-pots, when they

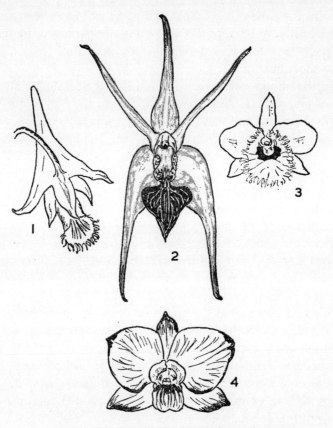

(1) *Dendrobium longicornu*   (2) *Epigeneium amplum*
(3) *Dendrobium fimbriatum*   (4) *Dendrobium phalaenopsis*

may be hung close to the glass and kept sprayed.

D. aggregatum. This has clusters of short, stumpy pseudo-bulbs, usually furrowed and wrinkled with age, with an evergreen solitary leaf growing from the apex. The flower-spike appears from near the apex, an arching raceme of deep golden-yellow flowers, often fragrant. It flowers during the spring and early summer and is best grown in shallow pans near the glass in the intermediate house.

D. amoenum. A slender plant with long thin pseudo-bulbs up to 2ft tall, which are completely deciduous. The fragrant flowers are produced along the length of the newest bulb and are carried in ones and twos. They are small, white, the sepals and petals slightly tipped with amethyst. The lip is white with a green throat. A cool-house species which will do better if any extra heat and moisture are available during the summer, and a decided rest is given during the dormant period. The plant is susceptible to red spider.

D. atroviolaceum. The hard, club-shaped pseudo-bulbs, up to 8in tall, have up to four broad, hard, evergreen leaves at the apex. The upright spikes bear up to ten drooping flowers. The sepals and petals are a creamy-white, usually heavily spotted with blackish-purple. The lip is pointed, the side lobes heavily blotched with violet on the inside, the outside being green. The flowers of this extraordinary plant will last many months in perfection. The species comes from New Guinea and is sadly very rare in cultivation. It should be grown in the hot house.

D. aureum. A short-growing species with smooth deciduous pseudo-bulbs, the flowers appearing in two or threes from the upper part of the bulbs. The sepals and petals are creamy-yellow and pointed, the lip a dark-brown to amber-yellow. This is an Indian species which is suitable for the cool house. The variety *heterocarpum,* although sometimes considered to be synonymous, has taller, more slender bulbs; the flowers are larger but paler in colour, otherwise similar. Both are very fragrant.

D. brymerianum. A most remarkable species with canes up to 2ft long or more, semi-deciduous. Flowers appear from the upper part of the pseudo-bulb in twos and threes; they are 2 to 3in across, with petals and sepals of a waxy texture, the whole flower being a bright golden-yellow. The lip is the most extraordinary to be found in all the Dendrobiums, being very large, and the greater part made up of interlacing filaments, forming a broad fringe. A rather scarce species from Burma and Thailand which should be grown in the intermediate house. It flowers in early spring (plate, p 108).

D. chrysotoxum. The furrowed pseudo-bulbs are club-shaped and up to 12in long. They bear two to three dark green leathery leaves at the apex, which are evergreen. During the late spring or early summer the racemes are produced from the top of the bulb with about six to eight blooms loosely arranged on the spike. The flowers are rounded and richly coloured in golden-yellow, the lip usually darker. Flowers in spring and early summer. A cool-house species which requires a decided rest.

D. densiflorum. A charming and distinct species with erect pseudo-bulbs 18in or more in height. They are broad, square at the top, and bear two to three leathery leaves, sometimes but not usually deciduous. The flowers, produced in dense pendent trusses, are of a soft papery texture, the sepals and petals curling slightly backwards. The golden-yellow blooms of this beautiful orchid unfortunately last only a week in perfection. The plant hails from Burma, is cool growing, appreciating extra heat during the summer when possible. It will flower from old and new pseudo-bulbs.

D. falconeri. The pseudo-bulbs are short and thin, and branch profusely from the ends forming a dense pendent growth. The plant produces many aerial roots and is best grown on slabs of tree fern or pieces of bark, and hung over a water tank where it will benefit from the extra humidity, as well as being kept sprayed. The bulbs are quickly deciduous, the grass-

Page 143:
Repotting a Cymbidium: (*above*) back bulb being removed: (*left*) old compost is shaken off and roots trimmed

Page 144:
Repotting a Cymbidium: (*above*) plant being positioned in new pot; (*right*) compost being firmed down

like foliage usually scarce. The blooms are produced in the spring; sepals and petals are white, richly tipped with amethyst, the lip is coloured with rich dark maroon with two orange blotches. Cool to intermediate house.

D. fimbriatum. The stout pseudo-bulbs, narrow at the base, are 2 to 4ft tall, semi-deciduous and well-foliaged. The blooms are produced in pendent racemes of six to ten loosely arranged blooms of a rich orange-yellow. The lip is beautifully fimbriated as the name implies. The variety *oculatum* has a dark maroon blotch in the base of the lip. This variety is far more common than the type. The plants will grow well in the cool house, flowering freely during the spring, after being given an ample rest during the winter. A most delightful Dendrobium (drawing, p 140).

D. infundibulum. Bulbs 10 to 20in high, the top half bearing several dark-green leaves which may sometimes be deciduous. The whole pseudo-bulb and especially the new growth and flower buds while young are thickly covered with short black hairs. The large, showy and very long-lasting blooms are produced in groups of two to four from the top half of the previous year's pseudo-bulb. The sepals are narrow and the petals very broad, the whole flower being pure white, except for the orange-yellow stain in the throat of the long-spurred lip, the flower vaguely resembling a Cattleya. The plant grows well in the cool house, but can be included in the intermediate house for the summer (plate, p 72).

D. kingianum. An Australian species whose habit varies considerably. The pseudo-bulbs are very broad at the base, tapering to a point at 10 to 20in, and bearing three to four dark green terminal leaves. The spikes, which are produced from the apex, carry numerous small flowers, which vary considerably in colour from almost pure white, through shades of pale pink to dark mauve, not opening fully. Although small, this

I

is a very pretty species which enjoys dryish conditions with plenty of light in the cool house.

D. longicornu. A plant similar in habit to *D. infundibulum,* the pseudo-bulbs being much thinner and more leafy. The long-lasting flowers, which appear in the autumn, are smaller, trumpet-shaped, and pendent, the edge of the lip is fringed with a few orange lines. This useful species is very free flowering, hails from Burma and grows very well in the cool house (drawing, p 140).

D. nobile. Without doubt the most popular and widely grown of Dendrobiums, this orchid is to be found growing wild over a wide area of India and as far south as Thailand and Vietnam. Species in cultivation today are usually of Burmese origin. The pseudo-bulbs are 18in or more tall, stout and fleshy with broad dark-green leaves produced along the whole length; they are semi-deciduous in cultivation. The flowers are produced in the spring from about half-way up the bulb to the top, in panicles of twos and threes where the leaves have been shed. Blooms are extremely variable in shape and colour (Frontispiece).

In the past there were several dozen named varieties. The typical colour of the petals is a pale rosy-pink, which deepens at the tips. The round lip is of similar colouring with a dark maroon blotch in the throat. The flowers are long lasting and sometimes fragrant.

This plant needs a decided rest for the winter, and may be grown in either the cool or intermediate house. It is sometimes possible that the season's growth may not be completed by the autumn, especially on specimen plants which have very tall pseudo-bulbs. In such a case one should proceed with resting the plant as usual, and recommence the growth in the following spring. Failure to do this may result in the lack of flowers for that season, and insufficient reward to the grower. Very few of the old named varieties are now available, but one in particular which is still sought after by enthusiasts is the albino form *D. nobile* var *virginalis*.

D. ochreatum. A short-growing Dendrobium, the pseudo-bulbs being curved and swollen at the nodes; a deciduous plant requiring a decided rest when not growing. The new growth appears in the late winter and develops quickly, the flower buds appearing from the axils of the leaves as the growth is completed, to bloom in the late spring or early summer. The blooms are of an intense golden-yellow, with a deep maroon blotch. Cool to intermediate house.

D. phalaenopsis (*bigibbum* var *Phalaenopsis*). A native of Australia which produces fairly tall woody pseudo-bulbs with foliage at the top. The spikes are produced from the apex and may be 12in long or more, carrying five to ten large showy blooms, often 3in or more across, which are highly variable in colour, from almost a pure white to rosy-pink and through to a deep rosy-mauve, while the lip is always a much darker colour. The petals are rounded and the lip is pointed. Flowering time various; intermediate to hot house, with a decided rest (drawing, p 140).

D. pierardii. An Indian species with very long, slender and pendent stems, up to 3ft long, most easily accommodated in a basket, and completely deciduous while resting. The flowers are produced for nearly the whole length of the dormant pseudo-bulbs, often in twos and threes and each about 2in across. The petals are a very delicate pink and the lip a creamy yellow. Very pretty and spring flowering. It prefers to be grown as warm as possible to obtain the longest canes.

D. primulinum. Bulbs thick and fleshy, completely deciduous, with upright habit 9 to 12in high, and foliage of a soft light green. The flowers are similar to those of *D. pierardii*, but the petals are rounder and appear in the late winter from the leafless nodes. Cool-growing and very fragrant.

D. spectabile. One of the most curious of all orchid flowers. The plant is tall-growing, with thick woody pseudo-bulbs bearing two to three thick leaves which remain on the plant for many years. The flower-spikes are produced from the nodes between the foliage, and bear six to eight of the most curiously contorted flowers, the petals and sepals being long and tapering, twisting all ways and wavy at the edges. The lip is similarly contorted. The colouring is basically a buff-yellow, streaked and veined with a dull reddish-purple. A rare but well worthwhile species for the intermediate to hot house, originating from New Guinea. Requires a definite rest when not active (plate, p 36).

D. superbum (anosmum). Produces thickish pseudo-bulbs of pendent or semi-arching habit, completely deciduous. The flowers are produced from the leafless bulbs in twos and threes in the early spring. The blooms are large, the petals long and of a rich rosy-pink, the lip more pointed with a darker centre. Lasting well and strongly fragrant, suggestive of rhubarb. It comes from the Philippines and should be grown in the intermediate house.

D. transparense. A tall-growing species from India and Burma whose very thin deciduous pseudo-bulbs attain a height of 30in. The flowers appear almost the whole length of the previous year's pseudo-bulbs and are carried in twos and threes. The petals and sepals are of a pale pink, changing to white towards the centre. The lip is blotched with a darker pink. It will produce a good display of bloom in the spring provided it has been given adequate light during the resting period.

D. victoriae-reginae. A beautiful species known as the blue Dendrobium. It may be grown upright in a pot or pendent on a piece of bark. The pseudo-bulbs are slender, swollen at the nodes, and branch considerably. They are generally deciduous. The flowers are produced at various times of the year. The basal half of the petals and sepals is white, while the tips are coloured and lined a purplish-blue. The lip is similarly marked. The flowers often do not open fully. Although not common in cultivation, it is very unusual, and being a high-elevation plant from the Philippines does best in the cool house.

D. wardianum. A charming species which produces pseudo-bulbs 12 to 18in high of a stout fleshy texture, with light-green deciduous foliage. The flower buds are produced from the top half of the pseudo-bulb in groups of two to three. The large flowers are white, the segments being blotched at the tips with rosy purple. The lip has a yellow disc with two deep maroon blotches in the throat. A very long-lasting and worthwhile orchid for the cool house. The variety *wardianum* var *album* is pure white except for the yellow disc on the lip; it is not so commonly seen as the type, and therefore greatly sought after.

D. williamsoni. Similar in growth to *D. infundibulum,* but shorter, the pseudo-bulbs having more foliage, and covered in dark-brown hairs. The blooms are produced from the top of the pseudo-bulb bearing foliage, with broad and pointed sepals and petals of creamy-white. The lip is pointed, with a brick-red centre. This scented and long-lasting species flowers in the early summer and is suitable for the cool house.

Epigeneium

This is a small but widely distributed and little known genus of orchids. For many years they were, and indeed sometimes still are, listed under *Dendrobium.* Only one or two species are occasionally seen in cultivation, which is a pity, as these are interesting and showy plants. The pseudo-bulbs are usually short and four-sided, of a hard texture and bearing a pair of short, stiff leaves from the apex, at the centre of which is the sheath from which the flowers are borne. The pseudo-bulbs may be spaced a considerable distance apart along a creeping rhizome, which produces very little root. For this reason they are best grown on long pieces of bark or a tree branch to which they should be affixed with a little moss. If grown in a pot a well-drained compost of equal parts moss and fibre is important, their culture following the same general lines as for Dendrobiums.

E. amplum. In this species the pseudo-bulbs are spaced 6in or more apart on a long upward-creeping rhizome. The flowers are produced singly in the autumn when the pseudo-bulb has made up, the petals and sepals being of equal length, narrow and pointed, basically coloured pale green shaded with brown or buff. The large, broad lip is white with a few markings on the basal half, the front lobe being a deep brown, or almost black. This interesting species from India does well when grown with the cool house Dendrobiums (drawing, p 140).

E. lyonii. A showy species with clustered, cone-shaped pseudo-bulbs of a yellow-green colour. The flowers are produced in long, drooping panicles of a dozen or more blooms. These are large and spreading with thin segments. The sepals and petals are a rich maroon or reddish hue, paling to almost white from the centre. Although not easy to obtain, it is nevertheless a very handsome plant and well worth growing in the intermediate house. A native of the Philippines.

Hybrids

The hybrid Dendrobiums are only second in importance to the species, which gives the grower all the variety he could wish for. Many of the primary hybrids were raised from *D.*

nobile and its many varieties, and other closely allied Dendrobiums. The present hybrids that have been produced from this strain are greatly improved, their large, perfectly round flowers resembling a miniature Cattleya. More recently a number of other species hitherto unused for breeding are being used to evolve new colour breaks and shapes, particularly in many of the hotter countries, where the tropical Dendrobiums can be more easily grown and flowered; and more interest is being shown in breeding from such species as *D. phalaenopsis, D. gouldii, D. schroderianum* and *D. taurinum.*

It is a little surprising that with such a very large range of showy species to choose from, more hybridising has not been done within this genus. There still remain many species from which nothing has been produced: the prospects of which are exciting, to say the least.

SUB-TRIBE GONGORINAE

Gongora

These plants are to be found throughout tropical America, usually growing on trees, where they may be in large clumps in fairly sunny positions. They produce oval or cone-shaped clustered pseudo-bulbs usually becoming ribbed with age. These carry one to three large, plicate leaves from the top. The plants closely resemble Stanhopeas, to which they are closely allied. The flower-spike is produced from the base of the plant, is pendent and may be up to 2ft long, bearing numerous flowers, these are curiously contorted and resemble a winged insect in flight.

These remarkable orchids should always be included in a mixed collection, and though their blooms seldom last more than ten days, they are rewarding for their fragrance.

The plants should be grown in a well-drained compost of three parts osmunda fibre and one part sphagnum moss, or similar well-drained materials in pots or slatted baskets, hung in the intermediate house. They will flower more freely when given a rest during the period of inactive growth.

G. atropurpurea. Produces long spikes in the spring or early summer which develop exceedingly fast and carry up to 30 or 40 flowers, each flower arranged exactly the same distance from the next. The basic colour of the petals is creamy white, heavily or lightly spotted with purplish-brown. The lip is usually a paler colour (drawing, p 168).

G. maculata. In this species the petals are somewhat more pointed than in the above, and the markings are finer, giving the flower a peppered appearance; the actual colour of this plant is also highly variable. It flowers in the spring.

Stanhopea

This genus of orchids includes species with the most incredible of flowers. They are distributed throughout tropical America where they are found growing on trees in similar habitats to the Gongoras. The flower-spike is produced from the base of the pseudo-bulb and usually penetrates the compost to emerge underneath the plant where it will produce a small number of very large, highly fragrant flowers. The buds develop quickly and the flowers will pop open suddenly, usually early in the morning. The petals are thrown back, exposing the large, broad column and the extraordinary shape of the lip, which together are of a heavy waxy texture. Their beautiful fragrance will fill the greenhouse, but sadly this perfection will last only two to three days!

The following species are all good subjects for the intermediate house, where they may be grown in well-drained composts in slatted baskets, so that the flower spikes can easily emerge through the bottom or sides.

Watering of the plants should be given careful attention at all times, bearing in mind that plants potted in this manner tend to dry out quicker. During the period of flowering watering should be withheld so as to avoid wetting the flower-spike.

S. eburnea. Scapes one to two flowered, blooms large and ivory-white with a fine peppering of purple. Strongly lemon-scented. Flowering period early summer. It hails from Trinidad and Brazil.

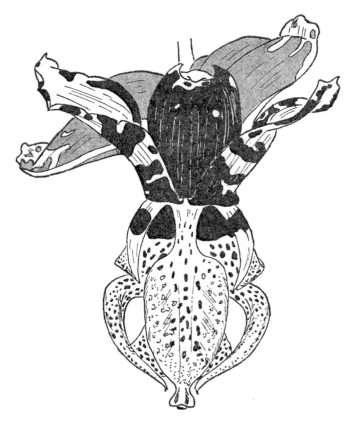

Stanhopea tigrina

S. tigrina. The most striking and popular of the Stanhopeas. Two to four flowered, blooms very large, somewhat variable in colour, the typical form being yellow, the sepals and petals

lightly or heavily blotched with maroon, while the base of
the lip, the column and the remainder are spotted a dull
purple. A native of Mexico, this species flowers during the
summer (drawing, p 153).

S. wardii. This species bears up to seven or eight flowers, sometimes more, which are smaller than the foregoing and vary
from yellow to orange, the petals and sepals being lightly
spotted with reddish-brown. The lip is paler with a large dark
blotch at the base. Flowering time late summer to autumn.

SUB-TRIBE HUNTLEYINAE

Huntleya

This is a very small genus consisting of plants with very
attractive star-shaped flowers, but only one or two kinds are
seen in cultivation. These are bulbless orchids producing tufted
growths of a soft light-green foliage, making very attractive
plants. The foliage is delicate and is liable to spotting if the
humidity is too high, or the foliage is sprayed too frequently.
They should be grown in the coolest end of the intermediate
house. Careful watering will be needed, the plant never
being allowed to become completely dry, at the same time
avoiding saturation and souring of the compost, particularly
if the plant does not have a large root system.

H. meleagris. A very handsome species which will produce
several spikes at a time in the later spring or summer, each
bearing a single bloom. The stems are approximately 6in tall,
and carry a large flower, with sepals and petals of equal proportions, about 3in across. The base is greenish-yellow, gradually changing to a reddish-brown towards the ends, though
highly variable in its markings. The lip is china-white, with
reddish brown at the end. The whole flower is of a heavy waxy
texture, and very shiny. The blooms are very long-lasting.

SUB-TRIBE LAELINAE

Brassavola

Although a very small genus this is important for breeding intergeneric hybrids. Brassavolas consist of modest-sized plants which resemble a typical Cattleya habit, with elongated pseudo-bulbs bearing a single leaf. The flowers are produced from the top of the pseudo-bulb. These plants are found growing in thick clumps in fairly sunny positions on the trunks and branches of trees from Mexico to Brazil, and are all best grown in the intermediate house. They should be potted in a well-drained compost of moss and fibre. During the growing season these plants will benefit from abundant supplies of water, but once the season's growth has been completed a decided rest is essential. The predominant colour among the species is green.

B. cordata. This plant bears long pencil-like pseudo-bulbs which carry a round, solid leaf, pointed at the tip. The flowers appear during the spring, in an inflorescence of up to six blooms. The star-like sepals and petals are a pale green, while the heart-shaped lip is white.

B. digbyana (Rhyncholaelia digbyana). This is by far the most important in this genus. It makes a large plant, resembling a Cattleya; the thick, stout pseudo-bulbs and foliage are of blue-green. The single flower emerges from a large sheath and is approximately 4in across, and slightly fragrant. The sepals and petals are narrow in proportion and of a very delicate green. The large lip is creamy-white, rounded and beautifully frilled. The species is most commonly found in Honduras and Mexico.

B. glauca (Rhyncholaelia glauca). The plant is more compact and shorter than *B. digbyana.* The solitary flowers are a pale green. The lip is white and striped with pink in the throat, without the characteristic fringe of *B. digbyana.*

B. nodosa. A small species from Mexico with short pseudo-bulbs and rounded leaves. The flowers are borne in threes and fours and can be up to 3in across. The petals and sepals are pale green with a contrasting white lip. The flowers are long-lasting and often fragrant. It has a wide distribution and can be found over most of tropical America (drawing, p 159).

Cattleya

This magnificent genus is without doubt the finest in this group. The species are wonderfully striking for their extreme richness of colour, their large size and fragrance of bloom. In addition they are easily the most widely grown plants in the orchid family, adapting themselves to varying conditions all over the world. In this country they are grown in the inter-mediate house.

Nearly all of them originate from the continent of South America where they are to be found growing on trees or on outcrops of rock, where their growth is somewhat stunted. When established in their native habitat the plants will live for many years, growing into enormous clumps many feet across.

The genus may be divided roughly into two groups. These are the unifoliates and the bifoliates. The unifoliate section consists of plants with club-shaped pseudo-bulbs which are joined by a creeping rhizome, spaced about 2in apart. The pseudo-bulb and rhizome are covered in a white papery mem-brane which is green in the new growth. At the top of the pseudo-bulb is carried a single large, broad, dark-green leaf of a heavy solid texture; from its base the flower sheath is produced. This consists of an oblong, pale-green envelope, which is almost transparent and through which the flower buds can be seen to develop. The buds will in time emerge from this protective covering to produce usually two large flowers.

The bifoliates have taller and more cylindrical pseudo-bulbs which terminate in a pair of shorter leaves and carry more, although smaller, flowers, of a heavier texture.

Cattleyas are best grown in the intermediate house, where they are so well known that this is often referred to as the Cattleya House. They are easy to grow, thriving in warm, airy conditions, and should be given a liberal amount of sunlight at most times of the year, although during the summer shading must be applied.

When the new growth starts in the spring and a new and active root system commences, watering can be applied regularly. In the autumn, when the pseudo-bulbs have made up and the root action slows to a minimum, watering should be reduced to allow the plants a slight rest.

Repotting is usually carried out in the spring, just as the new growth makes its appearance and before the new roots are active. These plants may go for many years without being repotted, and can often be seen with three or four pseudo-bulbs over the rim of the pot, while the plant continues to flourish and flower well! When repotting is undertaken the rhizome should be cut with a pair of secateurs leaving approximately four pseudo-bulbs. These may be potted up in a variety of different composts, which should be of an open airy material and be well-drained. At the same time 'back halves' or pseudo-bulbs which have been removed may easily be propagated in sphagnum moss.

It is well known that Cattleyas will withstand quite a bit of neglect, and do not attract red spider. However, they are very prone to attacks from scale insects, which build up their colonies unnoticed under the papery membranes of the rhizome and lower half of the pseudo-bulb. Such infestations should be swiftly dealt with by removing all the old sheaths as well as destroying the pest.

Cattleya hybrids often outshine the species, surpassing them in every way. For this reason not many of the species are found in cultivation today. Therefore we have listed only a few to represent this very wide and beautiful genus.

C. bicolor. This bifoliate species comes from Brazil where it grows at a great elevation on the trunks of the largest trees. The upright spikes carry three to four flowers which have olive-green petals and sepals with a brownish hue, while the unusual lip is reddish purple. Usually autumn-flowering.

C. bowringiana. Another bifoliate species which hails from Honduras. This is one of the most popular of the Cattleyas, being very free-flowering, with tall, slender foliage. The large heads of bloom with their rosy-purple flowers are a joy. The lip is similar but darker in colour. The petals can have a bluish tint about them, and in the variety *coerulea* the blue colour is quite pronounced (drawing, p 159).

C. citrina. A very beautiful and fragrant species. It has the extraordinary habit of growing downwards and is therefore more at home on a raft or in a basket. It has round, clustered pseudo-bulbs covered in a papery membrane. The single lemon-yellow flowers are pendent. The petals do not open fully but the blooms are long-lasting. This is a very high-altitude plant which is best grown in the cool house, where it can be hung up close to the glass and carefully rested during the winter. The species is most unlike the general conception of a Cattleya (drawing, p 159).

C. labiata. This species has many named varieties, which together form part of the group of Cattleyas already referred to as the unifoliates. At one time many of these unifoliate Cattleyas were considered to be varieties of *C. labiata,* but today are considered distinct species in their own right. However, the typical *C. labiata* flower can be as much as 6 to 8in across with large petals of a bright rose colour; the broad

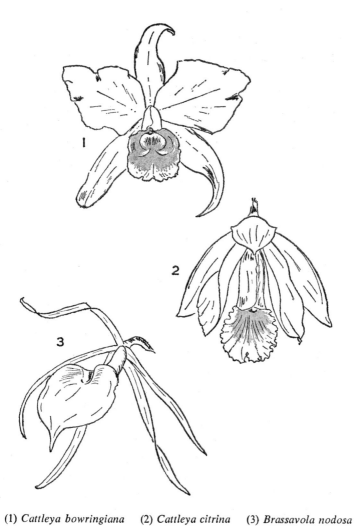

(1) *Cattleya bowringiana*   (2) *Cattleya citrina*   (3) *Brassavola nodosa*

wavy lip is deep crimson-purple with a yellow throat. It is long-lasting and very often fragrant.

C. mossiae. Generally considered to be a variety of *C. labiata,* the flowers are usually a little larger, with a more frilled lip.

C. skinneri. This species is similar to *C. bowringiana,* but is shorter-growing and produces larger flowers which are carried in clusters. The petals and sepals are rose-purple with a deeper lip. This species was originally found in Guatemala growing upon very high trees which made it difficult to collect. In the variety *alba,* the flowers are pure white with a yellow blotch in the lip.

Diacrium

D. bicornatum (Caularthron bicornutum). Only a single member of this very small genus is in cultivation today. It is usually imported from Trinidad or Venezuela, where it is found growing in very exposed areas on trees and rocks. It is especially curious for its pseudo-bulbs which may be 6 to 10in long and are completely hollow, usually with a small split at the base. The leaves are produced in pairs from near the top of the bulb and the upright spike from the centre. On a strong plant this can carry ten to twelve flowers, which are of the purest white; the sepals and petals are of equal size and pointed at the tip. The lip is narrow and pointed, and peppered with crimson-purple spots, with yellow in the throat. This species is best grown in the Cattleya house on a raft or piece of bark suspended in a sunny position. During the period of inactivity a good rest should be allowed. Although beautiful, this is a somewhat difficult orchid to grow.

Epidendrum

This is an extensive genus of epiphytic orchids, although

many of the species are of botanical interest only. There are known to be about 700 species in all, found all over the continent of the Americas, throughout the West Indies and out into the Pacific to the Galapagos.

Epidendrums produce their flowers from the top of the bulbs or stems. Their vegetative habit is extremely variable; from small round pseudo-bulbs with a thin creeping rhizome to tall reed-type plants taller than a man. Their flowers are even more variable, some bearing a single bloom at a time while others produce large, branched scapes. Or they may produce hundreds of flowers in continuous succession over a long period of a year or more. The colour variation and the combination of colours is almost without limitation; every colour can be found, white, green, brown to orange and red.

The plants are closely allied to the Cattleyas, usually producing smaller flowers which are often fragrant. It is the species which are grown today, little or no hybridising having taken place. Being a genus of such wide distribution and differing species, it is difficult to give general cultural information for them all, but some may be grown in the Cattleya house, while others may be accommodated in the cool house. A well-drained compost of moss and fibre will suit them all.

Among the Epidendrums mentioned here, as a general rule the bulbous varieties should be allowed to rest during the winter, while the reed type should be kept continuously growing.

E. ciliare. The plant bears a strong resemblance to a Cattleya, with stout pseudo-bulbs bearing one or two thick leaves. Up to six flowers are borne on semi-drooping racemes; they are fragrant and long-lasting. The petals and sepals are very thin and of a very pale-green colour; the white lip is well divided into three lobes, and deeply fringed. It is a widely distributed species but most easily obtained from Mexico, and grows best in the Cattleya house (drawing, p 162).

K

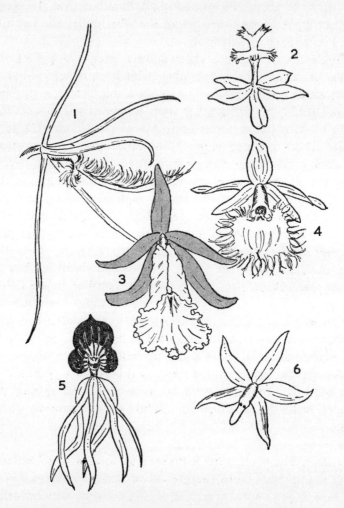

(1) *Epidendrum ciliare*   (2) *Epidendrum radicans*   (3) *Epidendrum mariae*
(4) *Epidendrum medusae*   (5) *Epidendrum cochleatum*
(6) *Epidendrum vitellinum*

E. cochleatum. Has large, flat, club-shaped pseudo-bulbs narrowing at the base, which terminate in a pair of dark-green leaves. The flower-spikes are erect and may produce up to ten flowers in succession, the first flowers being over before the topmost buds are open. The lip is carried uppermost, and is white in the centre covered with deep blackish-purple lines which suffuse to become solid around the edges. The petals are pale green and ribbon-like, hanging down in a twisted manner. It may be grown in the cool or intermediate house, where it will bloom freely without any trouble at various times of the year (drawing, p 162).

E. difforme. A short-growing reed-type Epidendrum with flattened stems and pale-green foliage. The flowers, three to four at a time, have thin petals with a large, almost transparent lip, which curls under. The whole flower is of a pale green, similar to that of the plant, and softly textured. An interesting plant for the intermediate house.

E. endresii. An extremely pretty species of dwarf habit from Costa Rica. It has short, reed-type stems, up to 6in high, with small dark-green leaves. The white flowers are carried in a cluster, the petals and sepals being delicately tinted with violet-blue. The lip is similarly marked with a darker colour. The plant, which should not be allowed to become too dry at any time, does best in a shady position in the cool house.

E. fragrans. A widely distributed and very variable plant; the pseudo-bulbs may be 3 to 6in high and compressed, usually bearing a single leaf. The flowers can number up to six at a time on an upright stem; they are pale green or creamy-white with the lip uppermost, this being rounded and veined with red on a white ground. It may be grown in the cool or intermediate house where it flowers in the autumn or early winter.

E. mariae. A delightful and most beautiful species from

Mexico, where it grows at a high elevation, mostly on rocky outcrops. The clustered pseudo-bulbs and foliage are olive-green and the flower-spikes are usually arching and can carry up to six flowers, which are large for the size of the plant, and long-lasting. The thick petals and sepals are coloured a beautiful lime-green, while the large frilly lip is pure white. It should be rested slightly during the winter, and grown in the warmest end of the cool house, where it will flower during the summer months (drawing, p 162).

E. medusae. A high-altitude plant from Ecuador which grows best in the intermediate to hot house. It is one of the most extraordinary of the Epidendrums. The stems are flat, about 10in long, and the fleshy leaves are set close together. The whole plant is of pendent habit, and should be grown on a piece of bark or raft where the heavy stems can be allowed to hang freely. A single bloom is produced, the petals being a greenish-brown and the round, predominant lip purplish-brown and deeply fringed. The plant should not be allowed to become too dry at any time, but kept in a shady position and kept sprayed (drawing, p 162).

E. parkinsonianum (*E. falcatum*). In this extraordinary species the pendent rhizome produces a thick dark-green leaf from a virtually non-existent pseudo-bulb. One or occasionally two large, pale-green flowers are produced from a thick stem. The lip is distinctly three-lobed, of an ivory-white. The plant makes a multitude of aerial roots, and is best grown in the inter-mediate or hot house on a raft of wood, allowing the plant to hang downward, where it may attain a length of up to 7ft. The species can be found all the way from Mexico to Panama.

E. polybulbon. A widely distributed species most commonly found in the West Indies. A plant of dwarf habit, never attain-ing a height of more than a few inches. The globular pseudo-bulbs are of a bright shiny green and bear two small leaves.

A single flower is carried upright; the very thin sepals and petals are a golden-brown, and in some varieties almost green; the large lip is almost pure white. In the wild this plant is to be found growing in the boles of trees or on rocks, the creeping rhizomes intertwining to form large mats several feet across. It is best potted in small pans and grown in the intermediate house, where it will bloom in the autumn.

E. prismatocarpum. The pseudo-bulbs in this species are stout and tapering, and bear a pair of long, narrow leaves. The tall spikes are carried erect, up to 15in high, with many flowers which are about 2in across. The petals and sepals are narrow, cream to pale green, blotched or spotted with purple, the small lip being rosy-coloured. A very pretty, fragrant and long-lasting species which will grow in both the cool and intermediate sections.

E. radiatum. A plant similar in habit to *E. cochleatum,* but the flowers are more like those of *E. fragrans.* These are borne on an upright spike, anything up to fifteen at a time. The waxy petals and sepals are thicker and more rounded than in *E. fragrans,* and the white lip is shell-like, lined with purple, The flowers are beautifully fragrant. It is widely distributed throughout the Americas and therefore variable. Will grow in the cool or intermediate house, flowering in spring and summer.

E. radicans (E. ibaguense). One of the most popular among the Epidendrums, which can be found in almost every collection. Noted for its free-flowering habit and succession of blooms which can last up to two years on a well-grown plant. It makes long reed-type stems with leaves carried alternately up the stem; specimen plants can reach 8 or 10ft high. This plant will look its best when planted out and trained up a wall or trellis where, with its vine-like habit, it will quickly make itself at home, producing numerous aerial roots. The plant also produces offshoots which propagate readily. The fine heads of flower are large while the individual blooms may be 1½in across, the whole flower being evenly coloured bright red. The lip is carried uppermost and divided into three lobes, the edges of which are fringed. The individual flowers are long-lasting and when finished are replaced by the supply of new buds which develop from the centre. It will grow in the cool or intermediate house. This is the most widely distributed of all Epidendrums in the wild, and therefore gives rise to several different colour forms (drawing, p 162).

E. vitellinum. A most noteworthy species in which the conical blue-green pseudo-bulbs grow in clusters. The flower scapes are up to 12in long, sometimes branched, with long-lasting flowers up to an inch across, of a bright orange-red, a flat even flower with a pointed yellow lip. It blooms during the summer and autumn and comes from Mexico. It enjoys rather dry conditions and should therefore be carefully watered during the resting period. Suitable for the cool house (drawing, p 162).

Laelia

The genus *Laelia* is fairly widely distributed but is mostly found on the mainland of South America from Mexico to Brazil. The plants from the north have rather stumpy short pseudo-bulbs with long flower-spikes while those from the south produce larger plants and shorter spikes, their habit closely resembling the Cattleya, with whom they are closely allied and will easily interbreed. The difference is mainly botanical, the Laelias having eight pollinia while the Cattleyas have only four. The southern species are best grown in the Cattleya house, while those from Mexico do well along with the Odontoglossums in the cool house. The compost should be of well-drained materials and a good mixture of equal parts moss and fibre will suit them. When the season's growth is completed, these plants should be given a decided rest. The flower-spikes are produced from the apex of the bulb.

L. anceps. This is a very elegant plant coming from Mexico. The pseudo-bulbs are stout and four-sided, with a single rigid leaf. A tall flower-spike 18-24in long is produced with two to three, or sometimes up to six, large flowers, which are 4in across. The sepals and petals are a soft rosy-pink while the lip is of a very rich crimson-purple with a yellow throat. This is the typical form of this species which varies greatly. At one time there were many named varieties which ranged from pure white to deep-coloured forms, but, alas, few of these are ever seen today. This plant is best grown in the cool house where it may be accommodated in large pans and should not be repotted too often. Resting in the winter in full light is most beneficial.

L. cinnabarina. In this species the dark-green pseudo-bulbs are narrow, wide at the base, and bear a single dark-green leaf of the same size. The flower spikes are carried erect, up to 10in long with numerous small graceful flowers a deep orange-red colour. It comes from Brazil and should be grown in the intermediate house.

L. gouldiana. A very fine orchid generally considered to be a natural hybrid between *L. autumnalis* and *L. anceps.* The habit of *L. gouldiana* is more robust and the pseudo-bulbs are taller than in *L. anceps,* and more rounded. The flowers are large, of a deep rosy-pink, with a lip of even deeper colour. A very attractive autumn-flowering plant, which is an old favourite (drawing, p 168).

L. harpophylla. This plant is similar to *L. cinnabarina,* but the pseudo-bulbs and foliage are finer and more slender. The flower is more orange than red. Culture similar.

L. majalis. Although more commonly known by this name

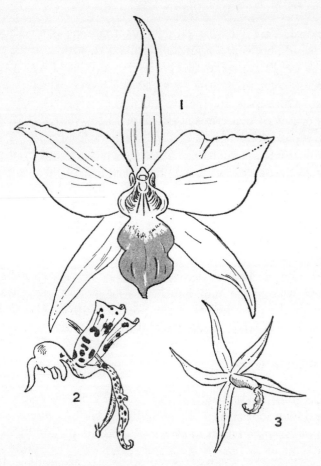

(1) *Laelia gouldiana*   (2) *Gongora atropurpurea*   (3) *Laelia milleri*

this is now considered to be *L. speciosa*. The clustered pseudo-bulbs, which are almost round, are wrinkled as a result of the very dry resting period it is subjected to in nature. It grows at high elevations in parts of Mexico and is best cultivated in half-pots or baskets. During the growing season it should never be allowed to become dry. The flower-spike rarely bears more than one flower, but this can be up to 6in across. It is fragrant, long-lasting and of a heavy texture. Although variable, the sepals and petals are of a rosy-pink, while the lip is very large, rose-lilac and streaked with purple. This can be a shy flowerer, and must be well rested with full light during the winter.

L. milleri. A dwarf-growing plant of more recent introduction from Brazil; the stumpy pseudo-bulbs are conical bearing a single hard leaf, of a dark reddish-green. The flower-spikes carry five to six blooms of a similar colour to *L. cinnabarina,* but the petals are usually wider and of a much brighter red, the whole flower being evenly coloured. Grow in a half-pot or pan in the intermediate house (drawing, p 168).

L. pumila. A compact species of dwarf habit, for the cool house. The pseudo-bulbs are slender and carry a single leaf. The large single bloom is borne on a short stem; the petals are broader than the sepals which overlap each other. The colour is a clear lilac-pink. The trumpet-shaped lip is blotched with a darker colour and yellow in the throat (plate, p 72).

L. tenebrosa. A stout, tall-growing plant with long pseudo-bulbs and a single dark-green leaf. Two to three flowers, seldom more; the reddish-brown sepals and petals are twisted, and lighter at the edges. This intermediate-house orchid flowers mostly in the late spring.

L. xanthina. A tall-growing plant closely resembling a Cattleya. It produces two to three blooms which are up to 3in across. The colour may vary from a clear yellow to a buff yellow, except for the edge of the lip which is white streaked with crimson.

Leptotes

A very small genus of miniature plants originating from

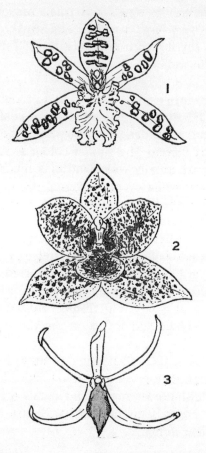

(1) *Helcia sanguinolenta*   (2) *Promenae stapelioides*   (3) *Leptotes bicolor*

Brazil. Only two can be found in popular cultivation today. These plants do best when grown in small pans or on blocks of wood suspended near the glass in the Cattleya house where they will flower freely during the spring months, producing large showy flowers for the size of the plant, which resembles a small Brassavola. The much reduced pseudo-bulb bears a single cylindrical dark-green leaf, with the flowers produced from the apex. Although the plants do not like to be over-watered, they should not be allowed to remain dry for too long.

L. bicolor. The larger of the two, bearing up to six flowers on a stem. The long thin petals are white, and the ends curl inwards slightly; the small pointed lip is violet. Sometimes scented (drawing, p 170).

L. unicolor. Perhaps the prettier species with small flowers, half opening, of a very delicate rosy-pink, the lip of the same colour.

Sophronitis

A genus of miniature orchids from Brazil, where they are found on mossy trees and rocks. There are several delightful species which are well worth growing, with large, gaily coloured flowers. The plants make very small pseudo-bulbs which carry a single thick leaf. When in bloom they are seldom more than 2 to 3in high and all do well in the cool house and occupy very little room on the staging. Grow these plants in shallow pans or half-pots in equal parts of finely chopped moss and fibre and in a shady position, where they can be kept evenly moist throughout the year. When grown on into specimen plants the Sophronitis really are a beautiful sight. Recently, this genus has undergone some rearrangement of its species and several of them have been reclassified. For the purpose of this book they have been listed under the names by which they are most commonly known.

S. cernua. Pseudo-bulbs very fat, with round, thick grey-green leaves. One to four flowered. Blooms small, sepals and petals of a cinnabar red, the lip of the same colour with an orange throat. Flowering period winter, when they will last a long time in perfection.

S. grandiflora (*coccinea*). Easily the most charming and best-known of this genus. Blooms perfectly flat, of a bright scarlet-red. The throat is orange-yellow. The long-lasting flower is produced in the spring, often 2in across, sometimes as much as 3in on a well grown plant (drawing, below).

Sophronitis grandiflora

S. rosea. Pseudo-bulbs squat with rounded blue-green leaves. The blooms are a rich rose pink with a tint of purple, and extremely pretty.

S. violacea. A more slender-growing plant, with pseudo-bulbs growing close together. The flowers may sometimes appear in twos, but more usually singly, and are of a dark-violet colour, which may vary.

Hybrids

By far the majority of hybrids in this sub-tribe have come from the Cattleyas, in particular those species which are grouped under the unifoliates, or *labiata* group as they are known, including *C. mossiae, C. trianae* and *C. warscewiczii,* to mention a few. This group of plants, even as species, are extremely showy and therefore were one of the first to draw the attention of the hybridist. Before long it was obvious that these plants would interbreed freely with closely allied members of the same sub-tribe, the Laelias, Sophronitis, and Brassavolas in particular, so that the hybrid of today usually has a complicated parentage of mixed generic blood.

The Sophronitis have perhaps contributed more to the hybrids, adding the brightness of colour found in *S. grandiflora* and good shape and texture of petals. From *Brassavola digbyana* come the large, frilly and open lips, while the Laelias are responsible for many of the colour variations. By using the albino forms of *Cattleya trianae* and *C. mossiae* the whites have led up to the most beautiful hybrids, such as *C.* Bow Bells and *C.* Bob Betts, which are the purest white with yellow lips. The more highly coloured hybrids such as the mauves, deep pinks, and two-coloured flowers with white or yellow petals and dark-coloured lips, are of such good quality today and so numerous that no names are mentioned here.

Although the majority of Cattleya hybrids have arisen from the unifoliate group, considerable interest has always been shown in breeding from the bifoliates and intercrossing the two. These hybrids are now becoming more popular for their new shapes and quantity of bloom. One of the earliest crosses raised was *C. bowringiana* var *violacea* crossed with *C. labiata* var *coerulea,* producing Portia Coerulea and first registered in 1907. This was one of the most interesting crosses for it helped to produce the pale-blue and mauve-blue Cattleyas, and it is disappointing that the blue line of breeding was never followed to any extent.

When several genera are intercrossed, the names are abbreviated into one, i.e. *Sophrolaeliocattleya*. However, when more genera are interbred such as *Sophronitis, Brassavola, Cattleya* and *Laelia*, the resulting man-made genus is called a *Potinara*.

Apart from the Cattleyas, little or no hybridising of note has been done within the other genera of this sub-tribe, and their importance lies in their use for intercrossing with Cattleya blood. Epidendrums were being used for breeding as long ago as 1890, when Veitch crossed *E. radicans* with *Sophronitis grandiflora* to give *Epiphronitis* Veitchi. This plant is still available today! A few other hybrids were made but in more recent years Epidendrums are proving to be of more interest in producing novelty crosses, again with Laelias and Cattleyas in particular. Today other allied genera such as Diacrium and Broughtonia are being crossed with Laelias and Cattleyas to produce even more new and interesting novelties to delight the orchidist.

SUB-TRIBE LYCASTINAE

Anguloa

This is a comparatively small genus of about ten species, which are closely allied to the Lycastes. They are found mostly at high altitudes in the Andes, and are mostly terrestrial in habit. They are robust growers producing large plants which make stout oval pseudo-bulbs and carry a pair of broad, plicate leaves of a thin texture, which are sometimes deciduous. The buds usually appear at the same time as the new growth, both developing together from the base. The flowers are borne singly on tall upright stems, depending upon the species, and several spikes may appear at a time. The petals and sepals do not open fully but form a cup-shaped flower, looking something like a tulip. Inside, encircled by the thick heavy petals, is the lip, which is lightly hinged at the base, enabling it to be rocked freely to and fro when the flower is moved, giving rise to the popular name of 'cradle orchid'. These blooms are long-lasting and noted for their scent. The species are all greatly sought after, but unfortunately rather rare.

Their general culture is very similar to that required by the more commonly grown Lycastes, and this is covered more fully under that genus.

A. clowesi. Probably the most popular of the Anguloas, with large, fragrant flowers of a beautiful golden-yellow. Two, three or up to half a dozen spikes are produced on a specimen plant. This spring-flowering orchid comes from Columbia and should be grown in the warmest end of the cool house.

A. rueckeri. This species makes a slightly smaller plant. The outside of the flower is a yellowish-green, while inside it is densely striped and spotted, although that differs from plant to plant. Flowering in spring or early summer, it is a cool-house species from Columbia.

A. uniflora (*A. virginalis*). The plant is typical of the genus, with tall, elegant foliage. The blooms are white, delicately spotted and flushed with pink. Flowering period early summer. Occasionally seen is the albino form, with its flowers of pure white. Best suited to the intermediate house (plate, p 17).

Bifrenaria

This is a small genus of attractive epiphytic orchids, the species of which are found mostly in Brazil. The plants produce hard robust pseudo-bulbs with a single stout plicate leaf carried stiffly erect. The flower spikes are produced from the base of the bulbs; the flowers may be single in some species, or several to a spike in others. These are always fragrant and long-lasting. The plants do best placed at the warmest end of

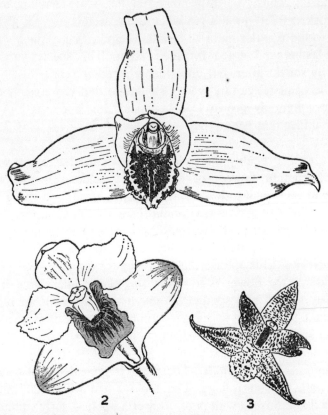

(1) *Lycaste skinneri*   (2) *Bifrenaria tyranthina*   (3) *Maxillaria tenuifolia*

the cool house, and should be potted in a compost of equal parts moss and fibre, or similar materials. The plants should be given a decided rest when growth has been completed, after which the flowers will follow in the spring or early summer. During the growing season they will enjoy a moist atmosphere, although overhead spraying is not recommended.

B. harrisoniae. This is the most common of the Bifrenarias. The flowers are borne on short upright spikes, one to two flowered. The sepals and petals are of almost equal size, producing round fleshy flowers of a creamy-white. The lip is rounded, covered in short hairs, and coloured a dark reddish-purple.

B. tyranthina. The habit resembles that of *B. harrisoniae* when not in flower. It usually has more flowers to a spike, larger and more highly coloured. The petals and sepals are shaded with a rich rosy-pink, and the lip is a deep reddish-purple; the colour may vary (drawing, p 176).

Lycaste

This is a genus of showy and long-lasting orchids which are distributed widely throughout central America. There are a little over thirty named species in the group. The plants may be terrestrial or epiphytic and grow mostly at high altitudes. The plants, while varying in size, all produce dark-green pseudo-bulbs which bear a pair of large, soft green plicate leaves, deciduous in most of the species. The flowers are produced singly on a stem from the base of the bulb, often a dozen or more blooms at a time. In the typically shaped bloom the sepals are large while the petals are smaller, often not opening fully. The lip is small in proportion to the rest of the flower.

The plants will grow well in a compost of moss and fibre to which may be added loam or peat to make a slightly heavier mixture. During the active season the growth usually develops quite quickly, and therefore the plants should be given an abundance of water, never being allowed to dry out. During this period of fast growth, it will be beneficial to add some liquid fertiliser when watering. A moist, shady position in the cool or intermediate house will be suitable, and ventilation may be freely applied, but at no time should the foliage be sprayed.

In the autumn when the growth is completed the leaves often develop brown markings prior to dropping off. The plants should now be rested until the new growth appears in the

L

spring. During this period of rest most of them will flower. At this time all water should be withheld and the plants kept in a slightly drier atmosphere, otherwise the buds may be affected by damping off.

It may happen that a particular Lycaste or Anguloa starts its growth in the autumn instead of the spring. When this happens the routine culture should be followed, regardless of the time of year. The plant should thus be watered throughout the winter and encouraged to grow; not forgetting that during the summer this plant will probably be at rest!

These are easy orchids for the beginner, being good growers that flower freely.

L. aromatica. The dark-green pseudo-bulbs are rounded and flattened. When the foliage is shed several thorny spikes are left on the top of the bulb. The whole flower is a bright orange-yellow and very fragrant. A native of Mexico for the cool house.

L. cruenta. The habit is similar to that of *L. aromatica,* with flowers usually larger, and not in so great a profusion. The flower is bright yellow with a dark-red blotch at the base of the lip. Cool house.

L. deppei. The sepals are long and narrow and sharply pointed. The basic colour is pale green, the sepals densely peppered with reddish-brown. The small petals are pure white and the lip is bright yellow, with a few red spots. A very striking plant from Mexico, which comes into flower in the early spring. Suitable for the cool house.

L. skinneri (L. virginalis). One of the most popular of the Lycastes, and indeed of all orchids. The beautiful flowers are very large, the sepals curling back at their tips. The flower is white, suffused to a greater or lesser degree with a rosy pink. The petals are of the same colour and are heavily marked with deep-rose spots at the base. The lip is white spotted with crimson. The variety *alba* has pure white flowers and is greatly sought after. There are a number of other named varieties, seldom seen today, where the colour varies greatly. Flowers during the winter. Cool house (drawing, p 176).

Hybrids

In this sub-tribe only a few crosses have been made to date, but no doubt one may anticipate steps forward in the future. By far the greater number of crosses have been made in the Lycastes, and probably the most exciting was the bigeneric cross between *Anguloa clowesi* and *Lycaste imschootiana,* which produced *Angulocaste* Apollo, which in turn when crossed with *Lycaste* Sunrise gave *Angulocaste* Olympus. These two hybrids have been highly acclaimed and awarded.

SUB-TRIBE MAXILLARINAE

Maxillaria

This is a large genus with something in the region of 300 species, with a wide distribution throughout tropical America. The largest concentration of these is in Brazil, where they grow mostly as epiphytes. The plants are highly variable and may consist of clustered pseudo-bulbs with one or a pair of leaves, or small creeping plants with grass-like foliage atop small pseudo-bulbs, as well as species with thick leathery leaves where the pseudo-bulbs are almost non-existent. The blooms are always produced singly from the base of the plant. While many of the species are large and showy, quite a number are merely of botanical interest. The flowers bear a close resemblance to those of Lycastes and Bifrenarias, and were at one time considered to be of the same genera.

It is difficult to generalise on the culture of these plants, their species being so diverse. However, the majority of them are not difficult to grow, and may be recommended to the amateur for the cool house. A compost similar to that for Lycastes will suit them well, but being epiphytes they prefer a well-drained mixture. Many of them will be suitably accommodated in small pans or half-pots, suspended in a fairly sunny position close to the glass. A decided winter's rest is needed by most of them, to ensure successful flowering.

M. grandiflora. Small flattish pseudo-bulbs which carry a single large leaf up to 18in long. The flower spikes are 7 to 8in long, bearing a large white flower about 3in across. The centre of the lip is yellow and the sides are striped with crimson. This plant usually blooms in the spring, and being a high-altitude species from Ecuador grows well in the cool house.

M. longispala. Has small rounded pseudo-bulbs. The extended sepals and petals are narrow, and may be 3 or 4in long. The flower is translucent grey-green in the centre, fading out to a soft pink at the tips. The smaller lip is pale yellow. An attractive species with its large flowers, though not always easily obtained. It originates from Venezuela and does well in the cool house.

M. picta. A very popular species noted for its strong perfume, which is particularly nice in the early part of the day. The pseudo-bulbs grow in clusters, are ribbed with age and with one or two strap-like leaves. On a well-grown plant it will produce many blooms about 2in across. The creamy-yellow sepals and petals are slightly incurving and heavily textured and the petals are marked outside with reddish-purple. This cool-house species comes from Brazil and may flower at various times.

M. sanderiana. The finest of the Maxillarias, coming from Ecuador. The plant grows to a height of 18in. The flower spikes are produced almost horizontally, and the blooms may be 6in across, with pure white petals and sepals striped and spotted with reddish-purple, particularly at the base. The lip is similarly marked with yellow in the centre. Unfortunately this lovely orchid is scarce today.

M. tenuifolia. Has small rounded pseudo-bulbs borne at intervals on an ascending rhizome, making a good subject for bark culture. The flowers are borne on short stems. The basic colour is yellow, the sepals and petals heavily marked and spotted with deep red. In some forms the red may become almost solid at the tips of the petals (drawing, p 176).

SUB-TRIBE ONCIDINAE

Ada

A. aurantica. This is the only species of this very small but delightful genus to be found in cultivation today; there is in any case only one other. The plant resembles the Odontoglossums, with which it may quite easily be grown in the cool house, requiring the same compost and conditions. The plant is shorter and more heavily foliaged than the Odontoglossums. The flower-spike is produced from inside the leaf bracts, and carries a dense spray of small, gaily coloured flowers. These are a bright shade of orange, the petals and sepals being narrow and pointed, the flowers opening about half-way. This species is spring flowering and has been used a little for bigeneric hybrids with Odontoglossums.

Aspasia

A. lunata. This is another very small and not so well known genus of epiphytic orchids from tropical America. They should be grown in the intermediate house and treated like Brassias. They are probably becoming more important today owing to their readiness to intercross with other genera of the same subtribe. The single flowers of this species are star-shaped, with narrow petals of a pale green, sometimes barred with chocolate. The spreading lip is white, lightly marked with purple.

A. variegata. The plant is smaller and the single flowers are greenish, the sepals and petals having brownish lines, while the larger lip is white, slightly spotted with violet. It hails from Trinidad, is summer flowering and strongly scented (drawing, p 186).

Brassia

The Brassias differ from the Oncidiums, to which they are closely allied, by their very long thin petals and sepals which give the flower a spidery effect. This, combined with their strong fragrance, accounts for their popularity. It is a widely distributed genus, found throughout tropical America, containing about thirty species. Most of these are easy to grow and free-flowering in the cool or intermediate houses, where they may be given similar treatment to the Oncidiums.

This genus has been rather neglected by the hybridist until latter years but is now being used more and more for making bigeneric crosses. These are hybrids of great potential not yet fully explored.

Most of the Brassias conform to a basic characteristic shape, differing mainly in their colour and size.

B. elegantula. A dwarf species from Mexico with short foliage and small pseudo-bulbs, the base of the plant being shaded with reddish-brown. The flowers are carried on a short upright spike no more than 6in high, with petals and sepals about an inch across. They are greenish marked with brown bars, and the lip is white with a few spots. It flowers freely in the summer, and should be grown in the intermediate house.

B. lawrenceana. A very striking species for the intermediate house. The plant is robust and bears long spikes with the very fragrant flowers well spaced out; their narrow petals can be up to 7in long. The segments are of a golden-brown spotted with reddish-brown. The heart-shaped lip is white with a few spots.

B. verrucosa. Has pseudo-bulbs more rounded, and stouter leaves, than the previous species. The petals and sepals are of a pale yellow-green, darker towards the centre of the flower, largely spotted with darker green. The lip is creamy-white and spotted. Another very fragrant species which is very easy to grow in the cool house, and which appreciates a slight rest during the winter months.

Cochlioda

Only a few species go to make up this charming little genus native to the Andes, where they flourish at a high elevation. Odontoglossum conditions suit them well, the plants resembling this allied genus closely. They are best known for their great contribution to hybridising where they have been used extensively in making intergeneric crosses with Odontoglossums, Oncidiums and Miltonias. There are only three species to be found in present cultivation, all of them beautiful.

C. noetzliana. A neat, compact plant. The base of the leaves and pseudo-bulbs are covered in reddish-brown, while the remainder of the foliage is dark green. The flower-spike is arching and may be between 6 and 12in long, carrying up to a dozen brilliant flowers, often an inch across. The slightly reflexed sepals and petals and the lip are orange-scarlet, with a yellow disc on the lip (drawing, p 186).

C. rosea. Similar to the above in habit; the flowers are more rosy in colour, with a distinct white column, and the flower slightly smaller.

C. sanguinea (Symphyglossum sanguineum). The flowers, which do not open fully, are borne on drooping racemes, very often two to a pseudo-bulb and sometimes branched, when the plant is strong enough. A rosy-pink and evenly coloured, the buds from the end of the spike are the first to open.

Miltonia

Very few of the Miltonia species are grown now, the beautiful showy hybrids having taken their place. The hybrid with which we are familiar is a highly coloured, pansy-shaped flower, with a large flat lip and 'mask' of contrasting colour. The most frequent colours found in Miltonias are rich dark reds, soft pale pinks and whites, with a few pale yellows, and every shade in between. The plants usually carry three to four blooms on a stem and while these will last a considerable time on the plant, they wilt very soon after being cut and put in water.

The typical plant has the Odontoglossum habit but with more foliage and smaller pseudo-bulbs, the foliage being blue-green and of softer texture.

Many of the species are very different from the modern hybrids. At one time great confusion existed as to which genus these species should belong to. For many years some of them were erroneously placed among the Oncidiums, Odontoglossums and Brassias.

Most of the Miltonias come from Brazil and Columbia with a few from other South American countries. Like the Odontoglossum, they grow best in the cool house, although they will benefit from being a few degrees higher during the winter. They should be kept evenly watered, never allowed to become too dry at the roots. Their leaves being soft, particular attention should be paid to the shading, also ensuring that the humidity is never too high, especially when temperatures are low. This will quickly cause spotting of the foliage. Although not considered to be ideal orchids for the beginner, when success with Odontoglossums has been achieved they make a good second choice, adding variety and colour to any collection. Similar culture to Odontoglossums will suit them, with the same type of compost.

M. endresii. This plant has flat, pale-green pseudo-bulbs which are well foliaged, with pale blue-green leaves, typical of the type. The short flower-spikes carry two to five large, flat flowers. The sepals and petals are white with a maroon blotch at their base. The lip is broad, white, and similarly marked, with a bright yellow crest. It blooms at various times.

M. flavescens. This is a pretty species from Brazil. The pseudo-bulbs are borne at intervals along a creeping rhizome which is often vertical, making this plant an ideal subject for bark culture. The pseudo-bulbs are long and narrow, bearing two narrow leaves all of a pale yellowy-green, which is the natural colour, and should not be mistaken by the beginner as a sign of ill-health. The upright flower-spike is 12 to 18in long, and may carry eight to ten flowers, evenly spaced down each side of the stem. When the flowers open they are coloured a very delicate pale green which tones to a creamy-yellow. Star-shaped, they have a small lip which is marked with purple at the base. This plant should be given a slight rest during the winter, after flowering in the autumn.

M. spectabilis. Similar to the previous species but shorter, with yellowish-green pseudo-bulbs at intervals along a creeping rhizome. The flowers are produced singly, or occasionally in pairs, and are extremely variable in their colour, giving rise to quite a few very fine named varieties. The typical flower is large and flat; the petals and sepals are white with a tint of rosy-purple. The spreading lip is of a much darker colour, and boldly lined. Summer-flowering (drawing, p 186).

M. vexillaria. Resembles the habit of *M. endresii*, with pale-green foliage and many leaves to a pseudo-bulb. The flower-spikes are tall and may carry six or more flowers, often several spikes to a bulb. The large, pansy-shaped flowers have petals and sepals of bright rose colour, while the lip is a richer rose, whitish at the base, and streaked with yellow and red. This colouring is typical of the species which may differ from white

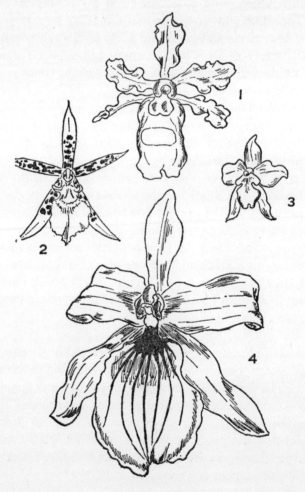

(1) *Miltonia warscewiczii* (2) *Aspasia variegata* (3) *Cochlioda noetzliana*
(4) *Miltonia spectabilis*

to dark rosy-pink in its several named varieties. By using these different coloured varieties to advantage, many of the excellent modern hybrids have been developed from this plant.

M. warscewiczii. A very distinct species from Ecuador, which has long flattened pseudo-bulbs bearing stout leaves. The flower-spike is erect or semi-arching, sometimes branched, carrying six to eight flowers which are usually clustered together. The narrow petals and sepals are brownish-purple, tipped white, while the sides of the lip are curled backwards to give it a roundish appearance, the whole being a dark brownish-purple. Spring or summer-flowering (drawing, p 186).

Odontoglossum

The species and hybrids of Odontoglossums are among the loveliest of orchids in the world. They were among the earliest orchids to enjoy popularity and to be cultivated in this country, due both to their freedom of flower and ease of culture in a cool house. The plants are compact, a mature specimen not requiring much more than a 4 to 5in pot. Almost without exception they consist of a flatish oval pseudo-bulb from the top of which are carried, either singly or in pairs, their dark-green foliage, with two shorter leaves embracing the base of the bulb. As the new growth is completed, the flower-spike appears between the bulb and one of the basal leaves. This will grow into an arching spray 18 to 24in long with numerous flowers evenly spaced down both sides. The colour range and variations of marking are almost unlimited. The basic ground colour of most of the pure Odontoglossums is white or yellow with a yellow throat, and the petals and sepals may be heavily marked or overlaid with darker colours in an unending variety.

With a large collection of these plants it is possible to have blooms all the year round, particularly from the hybrids as they have no definite resting period and flower when their bulbs are made up, regardless of the time of year. As a bulb may take about nine months to complete its growth; it does not necessarily follow that the same plant will always flower at the same time each year.

The species of this delightful genus originate from the New World, from as far north as Mexico to Peru in the south; but they are mostly found around Columbia and particularly on the westerly side of the continent. They are very much at home in the high altitude of the Andes, growing between 6,000 and 8,000ft in the cloud forest regions, where the temperature is constant and the humidity always saturated. Some of the Mexican and Guatemalan species, however, grow in dryer conditions and require a definite resting period. Their culture may vary slightly from that suited to their cousins in the Andes.

It can be seen from these natural conditions that it is quite possible to cultivate these orchids under artificial conditions in this part of the world with very little difficulty, even though we are at a much lower altitude. An ideal Odontoglossum house has plenty of fresh air and an even temperature, avoiding all undue fluctuations, particularly on hot summer days. The plants will therefore do best at the warmest end of the cool house where a winter minimum night temperature of not less than 50-52°F (10-11·1°C) can be maintained. No direct sunlight should ever be allowed to play on their delicate leaves, for this can so quickly result in scorching, particularly in the early spring after long periods of dull weather. The humidity in the greenhouse must also be kept constant, but too high a level during the winter may cause spotting of the foliage, particularly at the leaf tips. Therefore spraying of the foliage is not recommended.

Odontoglossums like to be accommodated in small pots, and they will therefore dry out more quickly, and careful attention should always be paid to the watering, making sure that the plants are kept wet enough; otherwise the pseudo-bulbs will quickly shrivel, and will take a long time to plump up again.

If the plants are placed on upturned pots or on a slatted staging to allow a free movement of air around them, and have adequate ventilation applied whenever possible, they will flourish. Odontoglossums like to be firmly potted in a well-drained compost of equal parts moss and fibre, although the experienced grower will succeed well by using a peat and sand compost. Repotting should be necessary about every other year and is best carried out after the plant has flowered and before it has started to make its new growth. It will be neces-

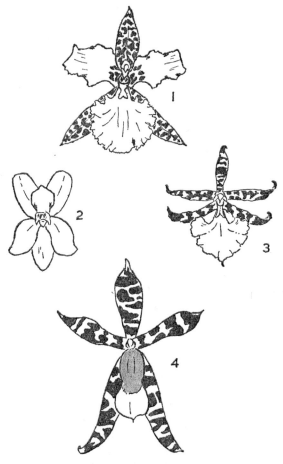

(1) *Odontoglossum rossii*   (2) *Odontoglossum pulchellum*
(3) *Odontoglossum bictoniense*   (4) *Odontoglossum laeve*

sary when the leading pseudo-bulb has reached the edge of the
pot. The oldest pseudo-bulbs may be removed to leave a plant
consisting of three to four pseudo-bulbs. Unlike the Cymbidium, the chances of these old pseudo-bulbs being useful for
propagation are very slight, as any eyes have usually deteriorated with age, and they are only fit for discarding. However,
should one wish to propagate from an Odontoglossum, it is
possible to do so, where a plant is large and strong enough, by
removing the leading pseudo-bulb and growth, leaving the
back half of the plant to start growing again. When this dividing is carried out on a strong plant, both halves will grow
without any obvious sign of check.

O. bictoniense. A well-known and very free-flowering species
from Guatemala and Mexico, for the cool house. On a well-
grown plant one may often expect three flower-spikes from a
pseudo-bulb. The upright racemes of flowers are 2-3ft tall,
sometimes branched, bearing many flowers which are basically
yellowish-green, heavily barred and marked with brown, the
heart-shaped lip varying from white to rosy-pink; the flowers
are sometimes fragrant. This is a very variable orchid which
has several named varieties, quite common today. It is robust
and easily grown, with pale-green delicate leaves and ovoid
pseudo-bulbs, which needs little or no resting period. It is
liable to flower at various times of the year, but usually during
the winter (drawing, p 189).

O. cervantesii. A very pretty dwarf-growing species also from
Mexico, which does well in the cool house. The ovate pseudo-
bulbs have a solitary leaf and resemble those of *O. rossii* in
habit. It flowers in the late autumn and will last in perfection
for many weeks. The flower spike is semi-pendent, bearing
five to six flowers which are white or pale pink with each sepal
and petal marked with a series of fine bars on the basal halves,
resembling a cobweb formation in the centre of the flower. The
almost plain lip is white, with a yellow throat.

After the growth has been completed the flower-spike appears from the base of the pseudo-bulb. During the winter, before the new growth appears in the spring, water should be reduced to give the plant a moderate rest. There are several named varieties of this species, varying somewhat in colour, although these are not often seen today.

O. citrosmum. A charming, sweetly scented orchid from Mexico, exceptional for producing long pendulous spikes. The plant has shiny green pseudo-bulbs bearing a pair of leathery leaves. Although not difficult to grow in the cool house, it must have a decided rest during the winter, when it should be placed near the glass to ensure maximum light. Severe shrivelling of the pseudo-bulbs may be allowed, as this plant is subject to this in nature, and it is indeed necessary to induce it to flower. In the spring when the new growth appears, watering may be recommenced, when the pseudo-bulbs will quickly plump up again. The spike appears when the new growth is very young and immediately plunges downwards, growing at a fast rate to a length of 18 to 24in. It may bear eight to ten large flowers of a pale delicate pink. Its flowering period is between May and July.

O. cordatum. A distinct and handsome species, widely distributed from Mexico to Costa Rica and suitable for the cool house, recognised when not in flower by the very flat pseudo-bulbs. The flower-spikes are erect or sometimes semi-arching, bearing many flowers with narrow petals and sepals which taper to a fine point. The colour is yellow, blotched and barred with rich chocolate-brown. The pointed lip is white with a line of brown spots down the centre and another round the margin. The flowering period is spring.

O. crispum. Originating from Columbia, this is a highly variable species and at one time some 200 varieties were known, their colours varying from pure white to pink-flushed, with plain or spotted petals, the lip similarly marked. Today, however, the genuine species is rather scarce, and one is more likely to obtain a line bred hybrid with a large round-shaped flower, of a pure crispy white with wavy edges and a flush of pink, especially on the reverse side of the petals. Apart from the occasional spot, the only other colour is the yellow throat. One of the few original named varieties still available is *O. crispum* var *xanthotes*. In this form the pure white petals and sepals are spotted with yellow; the flowers are smaller than the modern type.

This cool-house plant has no definite flowering period, and needs little or no rest. The usual green foliage may develop wine-red streaks when exposed to sunlight. This is not harmful, and is usually regarded as a sign of good health.

O. grande. This is without doubt the finest of all the Odontoglossum species, although it is sometimes considered not to be an Odontoglossum at all! It is a most showy orchid which no collection should lack. It is easily grown in the cool house, where it must be given a decided rest with full light during the winter months. It has stout, bluish-green pseudo-bulbs with thick leathery dark-green leaves. The flower-spike appears in the autumn and carries three to five large, gaily coloured flowers. The sepals and petals are a rich glossy yellow, banded and blotched with bright chestnut-brown. The small, roundish lip is creamy white and marked with reddish-brown. Owing to the man-like formation in the centre of the flower, it has become affectionately known as the 'Clown Orchid'. It comes from Guatemala (plate, p 17).

O. hallii. A pretty species from Ecuador where it grows at an elevation of 8,500ft, and is therefore suitable for the cool house. The plant has long thin pseudo-bulbs which bear two long leaves. The flower spikes are long, arching and branched. The flowers are pale yellow, with large chocolate-brown patches and spots, the petals tapering to a point. The lip is white, marked with yellow and spotted and fringed. Spring flowering.

O. laeve. A very elegant species from Mexico which bears tall, branched spikes of attractive, very fragrant flowers which are yellowish-green, banded and barred with deep chocolate-brown. The long lip is white, the basal half a rosy-purple. The plants make large, compressed pseudo-bulbs with a pair of dark-green leaves. It is a very free-flowering plant, suitable for the cool house, and should only be slightly rested during the winter (drawing, p 189).

O. pescatorei. A charming specie, similar in habit to *O. crispum*, but slightly smaller in growth. The flowers, which usually appear between April and May, are white shaded with rose, while the white lip is spotted with rose and has a yellow stain in the throat. It is a cool-house species and was first discovered in the oak forests of New Granada at about 8,000ft. It has several named varieties, all of them good.

O. pulchellum. A very neat and pretty species with thin oblong pseudo-bulbs, and two grass-like leaves. The fragrant flowers are carried on upright spikes, with the lip uppermost, and are small and roundish, waxy-looking, and pure white with bright yellow on the crest of the lip. This little orchid is easy to grow and never fails to flower in the cool house (drawing, p 189).

O. rossii. Perhaps the most popular of the smaller-growing Odontoglossums, this desirable little Mexican plant has small ovate pseudo-bulbs bearing a single leaf. The long-lasting white flowers appear in the autumn on short spikes, two to three together; the sepals and basal halves of the petals spotted largely with reddish-brown. The lip is heart-shaped, white or suffused with rose, often with yellow in the throat. It grows in the cool house, where it should be kept continually moist. The

M

variety *majus* is superior to the type and should be sought
(drawing, p 189).

O. schlieperianum. In general appearance this plant resembles
O. grande, the flowers being similar but different in colour.
O. schlieperianum has more flowers on a spike, which is up-
right. They are mostly pale yellow, banded with reddish-brown.
A native of Costa Rica, it flowers in the autumn and requires
the same treatment as *O. grande*.

O. uro-skinnerii. A very showy and beautiful species from
Guatemala and Mexico. The strong-growing plants have a
creeping rhizome and shiny green pseudo-bulbs which are sometimes spotted with purple. It is suitable for the cool house
and should be kept watered during the winter. The large
flowers, on upright spikes often 2-3ft high are chestnut-brown
mottled with green, the large frilly lip white flushed with rose.
Long-lasting, they appear mostly in the autumn when the
season's growth has made up.

Oncidium

This is a genus of great beauty showing a wide range of
habit, colour and style of inflorescence. The species are to be
found in the Americas, from as far north as the southern states
of the USA, in all tropical American countries and extending
down to the Argentine, as well as in many of the islands of the
West Indies. They grow from sea level to high in the Andes,
and from the dry almost desert conditions of Mexico to the
tropical rain forests of Brazil, adapting themselves to every
environment and thus producing many strange and different
forms to make up one of the largest genera of orchids; there
are over 700 known species. Many of them will grow
in the cool greenhouse alongside their cousins the Odontoglossums, requiring similar treatment. Others need to be
grown in the intermediate or hot houses where they benefit

from the extra warmth but very often require a lot more light to induce them to flower.

O. aureum. One of the high-altitude Oncidiums mainly from Ecuador, with soft green foliage and a pale-green pseudo-bulb. The flower spikes are tall and erect and sometimes branched, bearing several small, bright canary-yellow flowers of a waxy texture. The sepals, petals and lip are all of similar size, the lip being pointed. The flowering period is usually spring. It grows well in the cool house.

O. cebolleta. Remarkable for its foliage: almost non-existent the pseudo-bulb bears a large cylindrical dark-green leaf which grows erect to a sharp point and has a very hard surface. The flower spike is about twice the height, sometimes branched, and carries several flowers with a predominantly bright yellow lip. The smaller sepals and petals are marked with brown. Being a widely distributed species it is quite variable in flowers and habit. It should be grown in the intermediate house, where it will flower during the summer.

O. cheirophorum. A pretty dwarf species from Columbia which carries many flower spikes with small, dense, bright-yellow flowers which are sweetly fragrant. Several spikes can be expected from each pseudo-bulb; these are small and clustered. Suitable for the cool house, it flowers during the autumn.

O. concolor. One of the most attractive of the yellow-flowered Oncidiums. The six to eight large flowers are borne on a drooping spike, their main feature being the large lemon-yellow lip. The sepals and petals are very small in comparison and embrace the column. This is a cool-growing plant which flowers in the early summer, requires a slight rest during the winter and is sometimes slow to recommence its new growth. The plant has fairly small, dark-green pseudo-bulbs with a pair of dark-green leaves.

O. crispum. A remarkably handsome and large-flowered species from Brazil. The pseudo-bulbs and foliage are an attractive brown; the flower-spikes are tall and branched, with many flowers, giving an umbrella effect. The individual blooms are a golden-brown with a yellow margin and yellow in the throat. This cool-growing species flowers at various times of the year.

O. cucullatum. This cool-house species comes from a high elevation mainly in Ecuador. The flower-spikes are produced in the spring, and the flowers will last a long time in perfection. The colours are variable, from plum-purple to chestnut-brown, while the lip may be rosy-purple and spotted. There are several named varieties, which include *nubigenum,* which has a much smaller flower with an almost white lip, and *phalaenopsis* which is a much paler flower with purple blotches.

O. flexuosum. One of the most popular of the small-flowered Oncidiums, noted for the ease with which it may be grown and flowered in the cool house. The pale-green pseudo-bulbs may be spaced several inches apart along a creeping or upright rhizome which may be more easily accommodated on a piece of bark than in a pot. The flower spikes may be 18 to 24in long, are produced at various times of the year, and carry a dense mass of brightly coloured yellow flowers. The smaller sepals and petals are barred with reddish-brown.

O. hastatum. The pseudo-bulbs in this species are round and firm growing in clusters which produce a tall flower-spike 3 to 4ft high, branched at right angles to the stem. The flowers are 1 to 2in across; the sepals and petals are narrow, pale olive-green lightly marked with brown. A fairly small white lip is marked with a dark pink centre. This is a cool-house species which flowers in spring and early summer.

O. incurvum. The pseudo-bulbs of this pretty species are short and rounded, slightly ribbed, while the flower-spikes are tall,

3 to 5ft or more, taking on a graceful arch as they grow and bearing many branches which can easily carry over 100 elegant, sweetly fragrant flowers. The petals and sepals are thin and twisted, white heavily marked and spotted with rosy-pink, and with a white lip. The flower-spikes appear in the spring, taking several months to develop, the flowers opening by late summer. It is a good grower in the cool house.

O. kramerianum. Probably the finest of the tropical Oncidiums. The pseudo-bulbs are tightly clustered and flat, often very wrinkled and of a dark purplish-brown, bearing a single leaf of similar colour and hard leathery texture. The flower-spike may be 3 to 4ft long with a single bloom at a time. This lasts up to two weeks and is followed by another within a few more weeks. Left to itself, this succession of blooming from the end of the flower-spike may last for many months and even years; but this should not be allowed, as the plant will overflower itself to its own detriment. The flower is of a most extraordinary design: the dorsal sepal and two petals are about 3in long and held erect, while the lateral petals and lip are frilly. The whole flower is yellow, spotted and blotched with chestnut markings. This orchid, together with *O. papilio* to which it is closely related, are well known as the 'Butterfly Orchids'. They are plants for the hot house.

O. longipes. A pretty, dwarf-growing species from Brazil which has small, elongated, usually ribbed pseudo-bulbs with a single shortish thin leaf. Flower-spikes are short, carrying three to four flowers which are quite large for the size of the plant. The petals are chocolate-brown tipped with yellow and the lip is yellow. It is a free-flowering species which will take up little room in the cool house, flowering in the summer.

O. luridum. This species is widely distributed throughout the West Indies and parts of the continent. The pseudo-bulbs are

198

Popular Orchids

198 *Popular Orchids*

very small—almost non-existent—and the plant mainly consists of large, leathery leaves, 1 to 2ft high, of a dark green,
sometimes mottled with brown. In its native country the
leaves give it the name of 'Mule's Ear Orchid'. This plant will
produce a quantity of aerial roots. It should be grown in the
intermediate or hot house, where it will require maximum
sunlight without burning to encourage the flower-spikes, which
may be anything from 6 to 10ft long, branched, and bearing
many flowers 1 to 2in across in a florescence of old gold. The

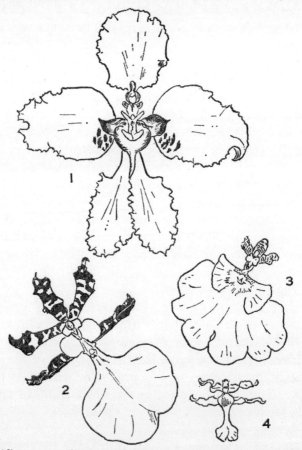

(1) *Oncidium macranthum*   (2) *Oncidium tigrinum*   (3) *Oncidium varicosum*
(4) *Oncidium ornithorynchum*

individual flowers are basically yellow, gently overlaid with blotches of a very light brown.

O. macranthum. Surely the most beautiful and spectacular of the Oncidiums, coming from a high altitude in the Andes, this is an easy plant to grow in the cool house. The plants are large and robust growers, with large pseudo-bulbs and plenty of foliage. The flower-spikes appear in the summer and continue to grow over several months to a length of anything from 10 to 15ft, with many branches. These are short, bearing two to three very long-lasting flowers each. The sepals and petals are club-shaped and of equal size, the petals being bright yellow and the sepals yellowy-green. The lip is white and comparatively small, with the centre a purplish-brown. The large petals and small lip form a typical feature of these high-altitude Oncidiums. The long flower-spike need present no problem in a small greenhouse, as it is very flexible while growing and may be trained into a hoop or circle between two supporting canes (drawing, p 198).

O. ornithorynchum. A medium-sized plant with oval pseudobulbs and plenty of foliage. It is a most desirable and extremely free-flowering species for the cool house, producing often three or four branched spikes per pseudo-bulb at a time, which may be arching or pendent. The flowers are small, most curiously shaped, and of a very pretty rose-pink with a small yellow centre. The massed effect of these little blooms on the arching spikes is most pleasing. The flowers are strongly fragrant and appear in the autumn or early winter (drawing, p 198).

O. papilio. The companion to *O. kramerianum* previously described. The flowers vary only slightly and are larger, with the upper sepal flattened in appearance. The lateral petals are longer than in the former and heavily marked with reddish-brown on a yellow ground, and less frilly. This plant requires the same conditions in the hot house as *O. kramerianum.* Both these plants require decided rests during the winter, and usually prefer to be kept a little on the dry side for the remainder of the year, needing a fairly light position in the greenhouse (plate, page 89).

O. pulchellum. A dwarf-growing species from Jamaica which bears several short narrow leaves of a hard texture, devoid of pseudo-bulbs. It is usually to be found growing on scrubby bushes in almost full sun. The flower-spikes can be 18 to 24in long, which is extraordinary for such a small plant. The blooms are comparatively large, although very variable, and consist of small sepals and petals which are dominated by the large rounded lip. The colour may be almost white suffused with a delicate shade of pink, to a deeper rosy-pink, with a yellow crest. This plant enjoys being placed in the intermediate house in a position close to the glass.

Oncidium pusillum

O. pumilum. The plant consists of short, stiff and erect clusters of leaves which are devoid of pseudo-bulbs, resembling the foliage of *O. luridum* but very much smaller. The scapes are upright, 6 to 8in tall, dense and branched, resembling a miniature Christmas tree. The individual blooms are very small, curiously shaped and coloured a bright yellow, sometimes spotted with reddish brown. It flowers at various times of the year, and should be grown in the intermediate house.

O. pusillum. One of the prettiest orchids to grow, this miniature Oncidium has no pseudo-bulbs and the foliage is arranged in a perfectly flat, fan-like formation. The new leaves are continually produced from the centre of the plant. The flower-spikes appear several at a time from in between the axils of the leaves, usually bearing a succession of single large yellow flowers, in which the lip is the main feature. The base of the petals and the crest of the lip are delicately peppered with red. The whole plant is no more than 2 to 3in high. It grows best in a shady position in the intermediate house, where it should never be allowed to remain dry for long periods (drawing, p 200).

O. tigrinum. An extremely handsome species which is easy to grow in the cool house where it is most free-flowering. The plant has stout pseudo-bulbs with dark green leaves. The flower-spikes are tall and branched with large fragrant flowers, of which the sepals and petals are yellow and heavily blotched with chocolate-brown. The lip, clear bright yellow, is large and spreading. These most attractive blooms will last for many weeks in perfection (drawing, p 198).

O. triquetrum. Another miniature species from Jamaica, the habit resembling that of *O. pulchellum,* but the foliage being a little redder in colour. The culture should be the same, in the intermediate house. The short drooping flower-spikes usually carry four to six flowers which are white, heavily striped and blotched in brick-red. A free-flowering little plant.

O. varicosum. A most beautiful plant for the cool house. The usually oval pseudo-bulbs grow in clusters and become shrivelled with age; they are usually peppered or spotted with purple-black. The flower-spikes are long and arching and may carry an enormous amount of flowers. The most predominant feature is the large lip, of a bright, intense yellow. The very small sepals and petals are yellowish-green marked with brown. It is certainly one of the most popular of the cool-house Oncidiums. The variety *rogersi* is superior to the type and greatly sought (drawing, p 198).

Hybrids

Odontoglossums, being the largest and showiest in this sub-tribe, have been used the most for hybridising. This started many years ago, at the end of the nineteenth century, and in those days when collections consisted wholly of species the hybridist had a wide choice of the best plants to breed from and to pursue whichever colour line he wished—*O. crispum* and its enormous variations and different colour forms for example, together with *O. harryanum* and *O. triumphans,* offered a wonderful start to what was to become a fantastic range of colour and shape.

It was not long before other popular genera such as Miltonias were being bred from as well, although the colour range is not so wide in this genus. There are many beautiful Miltonias, and the size and shape has been improved as well as the general quality of the flowers, with spectacular colours varying from dark red to pink and white with a few yellows of pastel shades. The Oncidiums have been bred from since the beginning, but not to the same extent as the Odontoglossums and Miltonias. Their main use in hybridising is in crossing with the other members of their sub-tribe to produce bi-generic and multi-generic hybrids, taking every advantage of their colour and shape to enhance the progeny. With all these multigeneric hybrids not only have we got new man-made hybrids, with new generic names, but we have also plants unlike any of their parents, with a completely new shape, colour and habit.

It is not new to intercross different genera: this was first done as long ago as 1904, when a milestone was reached with the creation of the first bigeneric hybrid, namely *Cochlioda noetzliana* x *Odontoglossum pescatorei* which, when exhibited for the first time, caused a sensation in the orchid world. The plant was called *Odontioda* Vuylstekeara and combined the size of the Odontoglossum with the brilliant colour of the Cochlioda. While pure Odontoglossum hybrids have been produced in their thousands, Cochlioda, on the other hand, has not been crossed with other varieties of its own genus, but has been used extensively for interbreeding mostly with Odontoglossums, Oncidiums and Miltonias.

Multigeneric hybrids involving three or four different genera are now quite frequent, and today the range is being made even wider with the intervention of the Aspasia and Brassia blood, giving rise to yet more shapes and colours previously unknown.

Naming these intergeneric crosses produced another problem. When a *Cochlioda* and *Odontoglossum* are crossed the result is called an *Odontioda*. *Cochlioda* and *Miltonia* gives *Miltonioda*, and *Cochlioda* and *Oncidium* is *Oncidioda*, to give a few examples. But when a cross involves three or more genera, such as *Cochlioda*, *Miltonia* and *Odontoglossum*, the hybrid is given the multigeneric name of *Vuylstekeara*, named after the originator of the first cross of its kind. Another example is Wilsonaria which is the result of crossing *Cochlioda*, *Odontoglossum* and *Oncidium*. The above are only some of the intergeneric crosses achieved so far; there are many others not mentioned, and no doubt there are many others to be produced in the future.

These multigeneric crosses are not achieved without careful consideration of the plants used, and their affinity to each other, and only after many crosses and a lot of empty seed pods is one's patience rewarded, sometimes with only a few seedlings to grow on. It is necessary in many cases to return to the species to obtain fertility of seed as many of the hybrids are barren.

The culture of these intergenerics is, of course, very similar to that required by their parents. Nearly all of them have been produced from the cool-growing species and therefore general culture as applied in the Odontoglossum house will suit them well. The plants are very often more vigorous than the parents and grow and flower quite freely. When it comes to propagating they have the advantage of being more easily propagated both by back-bulbs and division, and more easily meri-stemmed.

SUB-TRIBE PHYSURINAE

Anoectochilus

This small but outstanding genus comprises about twenty species, known collectively as the Jewel Orchids. They are mostly terrestrial or sometimes epiphytic, with a distribution throughout south-east Asia. Most of the species found in culti-vation today come from India and Burma.

Unlike the majority of orchids these plants are not grown for their flowers, but rather for their delicate and beautiful foliage.

The plants consist of a succulent creeping rhizome, the foliage arranged alternately along its length, ending in a rosette of leaves, from the centre of which emerges the flower spike. The small, unattractive, sometimes evil-smelling flowers are produced on an upright spike. It is better for these plants if they are not allowed to flower, as this exerts a considerable strain which may result in the loss of the plant. The velvety leaves may be coloured in dark hues of green or copper, and lined with a network of delicate veins in gold and silver.

Little or no root is made from the underside of the rhizome and this is usually very hairy.

It is to be regretted that these charming little plants are far from easy to grow, and tax the grower's skill to the limit. Their fleshy nature makes them most vulnerable to damping off and rot, and therefore opinions are divided as to the best method of growing them, particularly with regard to their type of compost. The following is one method with which we have had considerable success. The compost consists of sphagnum peat and sand in equal parts, with a small addition of finely chopped fresh sphagnum moss, and a sprinkling of dried cow manure in the base. A well-crocked pan should be used; plastic has been found most beneficial for the plants, allowing continuous moisture. The compost is placed loosely around the base of the plant, without applying any pressure and allowing the rhizome to sit on the surface.

The plants should be grown continually in the hot house where they may be given similar conditions to Phalaenopsis. Ideally they are placed under a plastic seed-tray cover, which should not be completely closed. Otherwise a small propagating frame will suit them well. This will protect them from any detrimental draughts, while allowing a small amount of fresh air. Shading at all times from the direct sunlight is most important. In our opinion this is the keynote to success, avoiding all extremes in temperature, light and humidity.

Once a grower has achieved success with Anoectochilus they will prove a most rewarding orchid, being a constant source of admiration and interest.

A. elwesii. The heart-shaped copper-coloured leaves are produced on a slender rhizome, and are crisped at the edges. No other colours appear on the plant.

A. hispida. Narrow, pointed and closely set leaves, on an upright stem, are of a dark bottle-green netted with silvery veins.

A. regalis. This species has larger, rounded leaves of a bronzy-green colour, with a delicate interlacing network of gold veins (plate, p 36).

SUB-TRIBE PHAINIAE

Calanthe

This is a large genus of very widely distributed terrestrial orchids, found from Africa to Australia, with the most important species coming from the Far East. Calanthes can be divided into two groups, comprising the evergreen and the deciduous types. The latter are the most important, being by far the more showy and worthy of being grown. Anyone desiring to grow the evergreen types should apply similar culture as that recommended for the Phaius.

The deciduous species make stout pseudo-bulbs up to 6in long, sometimes waisted, which carry several ribbed leaves of a soft texture, which should not be sprayed. The flower-spike appears from the base of the completed pseudo-bulb, and varies in length depending upon the species, but may be several feet long, bearing a head of showy, long-lasting flowers. The sepals and petals are usually small, while the long-spurred lip is large and colourful. The flowers are produced in succession.

Annual repotting is required by these orchids, when the new growth appears in the spring. The rich compost should consist of peat or loam with sand added as an aggregate and a liberal amount of dried cow manure, or something similar, in the base of the container. When root activity starts watering is increased, until at the height of summer the plants are receiving liberal amounts, keeping them continually moist, and are also being fed with a liquid fertiliser. The new growth develops quickly and the pseudo-bulb is completed by the autumn when the flower-spikes appear, and the leaves are then discarded. At this stage watering should be gradually reduced and finally withheld altogether throughout the winter. When the flowers have finished, the pseudo-bulbs may be removed from the pot, divided up singly after shaking off the old compost, and placed upright in a tray until ready for potting. The oldest pseudo-bulbs will usually grow again, producing a smaller one for the first year.

Whether these plants are growing or resting, they should be given a sunny position in the intermediate house. With their short, fast, growing season, they will enjoy high summer temperatures.

C. vestita. Of all the deciduous Calanthe species this is the only one to be found in cultivation today, and as it is extremely variable there are many different forms, and also many hybrids from it. The plant is typical, with long arching flower-spikes producing many blooms. The petals and sepals are usually white, sometimes slightly suffused with pink; the lip may be wholly or partly covered in deep rosy-pink. In other varieties the whole flower may be pure white.

The early orchid growers used this plant mainly for house decoration, and large displays of well-grown plants created a beautiful sight lasting for many weeks (drawing, p 208).

Phaius

This is a smaller genus than Calanthe, but closely related to the evergreen varieties, with the same geographical distribution. The pseudo-bulbs are small and rounded and usually enclosed by the base of the leaves, which are long and plicate. The flower-spike is produced from inside the first leaf and stands erect, well clear of the foliage, carrying a large head of flowers. They are best accommodated in the intermediate house, or hotter, and being terrestrial in habit benefit from a peat or loam compost with sand and cow manure added, which should be kept evenly moist at all times. During the summer months, when the plant is growing fast, watering may be increased accordingly. These plants are not deciduous and should be only slightly rested during the winter. At no time should the foliage be heavily sprayed with water, and a light airy position in the greenhouse will suit them well.

P. tankervilliae. May be known as *P. blumei* or *P. grandifolius.* This is an extremely handsome species with a wide distri-

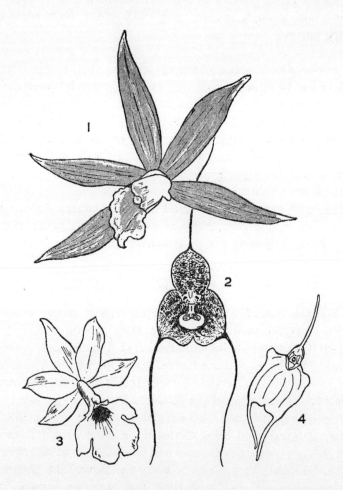

(1) *Phaius tankervilliae*   (2) *Masdevallia bella*   (3) *Calanthe vestita*
(4) *Masdevallia tovarensis*

bution throughout the whole of the Far East. Therefore a number of geographical varieties occur, causing it to be known under several names. The flower-spike will carry up to a dozen or more blooms, each up to 4in across, not all opening together. Usually, the first flower has finished by the time the last flowers are open. The outsides of the sepals and petals are a silvery white, while the insides are russet-brown with a yellow margin. The trumpet-shaped lip is white and coloured with rosy-purple. The usual flowering period is spring (drawing, p 208).

Hybrids

A number of hybrids in this sub-tribe were produced, most of them many years ago. Today this breeding has come to a standstill, and the only hybrids available are a few plants which have survived from those earlier days. These are mostly Calanthes, which were raised in considerable numbers around the 1890s. The first orchid hybrid ever raised was a *Calanthe* Dominyi, which is *C. furcata* x *C. masuca,* and was made by Veitch's in 1853. There were also a number of Phaius and Phaiocalanthe hybrids made about the same time.

SUB-TRIBE PLEUROTHALLIDINAE

Masdevallia

This large genus of orchids includes natives of South America, and while a few may be found in Mexico to Brazil, the vast majority grow in the Andes, in the cloud forest regions of Peru and Columbia, where they thrive in the cool moist atmosphere, growing on rocks or low trees. The plant produces a solitary leaf of a thick fleshy nature, from a short stem, being completely devoid of pseudo-bulbs. The plants continually divide, and very quickly grow into large tufted clumps. The flower-spikes grow from the base of the foliage; the stem may be as long as 2ft, or in some species virtually non-existent.

N

The flowers all have similar characteristics. The sepals form the main part of the blooms: these are broad and more often tipped with long tails. The petals and lip are very small and inconspicuous. Some brilliant shades of red are to be found in this genus, also soft browns and yellows, and one pure-white species. The blooms may be single or carried several at a time, or produced in a succession.

Cool-house conditions suit these plants admirably, where they may be grown in a shady position with plenty of fresh air combined with moist atmosphere. They should be kept watered throughout the year, never being allowed to dry out completely. Being without pseudo-bulbs, these plants do not rest, and should therefore be kept continually growing. They produce several new growths at a time, and are easily propagated by division, although they look their best when grown into specimen plants and accommodated in shallow pans or, with some species, baskets. A finely-chopped compost of moss and fibre will suit their fine rooting system. Even a well-grown specimen does not demand a great deal of room, and can easily be accommodated in a 3 to 4in pan.

M. bella. Has leaves 6in high, spikes pendulous at first, creeping across the compost in the same manner as a root. When the flower opens the bloom faces downwards, and may be tied up to be seen to full advantage. The flowers are large and triangular; the basic colour is white, densely flecked with brown, the long 'tails' are also dark brown. The small white lip is cup-shaped and loosely hinged. A succession of bloom is produced from the spike, which should not be removed until withered. A very neat and pretty orchid, which flowers freely throughout the late summer (drawing, p 208).

M. coccinea. One of the most beautiful and popular of the Masdevallias. Leaves up to 9in tall, flower-spike much taller, up to 2ft long, producing a large, single bloom, of which the bottom sepals are much larger than the dorsal sepal, forming a tube at the base which encloses the diminutive petals and lip. There are many named varieties of this species: they are all self-coloured, vivid and intense, and vary from a deep rosy-pink to blood red. This species from Columbia usually flowers in the early part of the summer (plate, p 53).

M. muscosa. One of the miniature Masdevallias and the most curious of orchids. The leaves are club-shaped, dark green, about 2in long. The flower-spikes are taller than the foliage and covered in dense hairs, except for a short length halfway up the stem. The flower is of a translucent yellow colour, the lip being somewhat large for Masdevallias, very unusual for its sensitivity, a rare occurrence in orchids. When an insect alights on the lip, the latter snaps up against the column, remaining in this closed position for about twenty minutes—a device to ensure pollination when the insect flies off to another flower.

M. simula. A curious dwarf species; the flowers are stemless, nestling among the short foliage, usually in quite a profusion of very small blooms. These are yellowish, heavily marked with reddish-brown spots. The lip is small and a dull purple.

M. tovarensis. Flower spikes 5 to 6in high, which may bear three to four blooms at a time, flowering for two consecutive years. The blooms are of medium size, the two sepals larger than the dorsal sepal, all with fairly short 'tails'. The whole flower is of a powdery white, and appears in the winter (drawing, p 208).

Pleurothallis

Over a thousand individual species constitute this genus, making it the largest group of orchids to be found in tropical America. The variation among the species is very wide, in both foliage and bloom, but nearly all of them make miniature plants resembling the Masdevallias in habit, to which they are closely allied. The leaves are usually carried on a slightly longer, slender stem, from the top of which the flowers are produced. The sepals are usually the most dominant feature of the flower, while the petals and lip are more often less conspicuous. Colours vary greatly, being often of a translucent nature. There may be one or two flowers, or long sprays of usually very small flowers, which in some species are produced in great profusion.While some of the species are very showy, by far the greater proportion are only of botanical interest. However, as they take up such little room, being grown in small pans hung close to the glass, they have a novelty interest, growing and flowering most freely. They require the same cultural conditions in the cool house as the Masdevallias.

P. minutiflora (*stenostachya*). Leaves very small, thick and rounded, dark green and speckled on the undersides. Flower-spikes erect, 2in long, extremely thin, carrying up to six minute blooms which are a translucent white, with little marking.

P. pachyglossa. Large roundish foliage carried on tall stems. The spikes produced from the base of the leaf with several flowers of a translucent pink or dull purple. Flowers late summer; comes from Mexico.

P. tribuloides. A plant about 2in high; the supporting stem is very short resulting in the flowers being produced low down, nestling among the foliage. Numerous blooms are produced in the late spring, of a brick-red colour.

P. ghiesbreghtiana. Leaves of medium height, with a brown sheathing at the base. Flower-spikes taller than the foliage, up to 9in long and many-flowered. Blooms set close to the stem, individually small and orange, attractive and long lasting. Variable. Comes mainly from Mexico and flowers in the spring.

SUB-TRIBE SARCANTHINAE

Aërides

The Aërides are widely distributed throughout the tropical countries of the Old World, although the majority of plants in cultivation in this country are from India and Burma. They are found growing naturally upon trees close to water, often maturing into huge clumps making an impressive display when in flower, filling the jungle air with their perfume. The plants make extensive root systems, the long white roots hanging down from the host tree and absorbing the moisture from the humid atmosphere. The name Aërides is derived from words meaning 'Air Plants'!

The habit of the plant is typical of this sub-tribe, having an upright stem with leaves alternately placed along its length. The new leaves are always produced from the centre as the plant progresses upwards. It is sometimes possible for side shoots to be produced, thus starting a new plant. The roots appear nearly all the way up this stem, and although very thick are brittle; they are white with a green tip when growing. The flower racemes coming from the axils of the leaves are usually pendent, carrying many medium-sized, very fragrant flowers. The sepals and petals are usually of equal proportions and waxy in their appearance. The lip is large, in proportion, and is curious for its shape, usually having a spur which curves upwards towards the front of the flower. The basic colours of these flowers are pink and white.

These plants are most suited to culture in baskets or, failing that, fairly large pots, when they may be grown in a coarse, open compost of well-drained materials, such as lumps of tree fern or bark when obtainable, otherwise three parts osmunda fibre to one part sphagnum moss. Once a plant has become established, it is better not to disturb it more than necessary. The different species may be grown in the intermediate house, where they enjoy shady, moist conditions.

Owing to their complete lack of pseudo-bulbs their only reserves are their thick fleshy roots and leaves. Therefore they should never be allowed to become completely dry. As they very often make more aerial roots than pot roots, it is beneficial to spray them at least once a day and preferably more often during the summer months, care always being taken not to allow moisture to lie in the central growth for too long for fear of it causing decay.

A. fieldingii. A species from the Himalayas which does not grow very tall. It bears narrow, dark-green leaves which may be up to 10in long, coloured a dark reddish-brown near the stem. The pendent spike, which may be 12in long, or more on a robust plant, is crowded with many rosy-pink flowers, while the basal halves of the sepals and petals are nearly white. The large lip is pointed and of a deeper but variable colour. This is an easy orchid to flower during the early summer, the blooms being long-lasting and fragrant.

A. lawrenceae. A tall-growing plant usually 2 to 2½ft high in cultivation, though sometimes taller in a specimen plant. The plant is typical of the type. The flowers are basically white, the sepals and petals tipped with rosy purple. The centre of the lip is similarly coloured, and the upturned spur is yellow. Summer-flowering (drawing, p 216).

A. odoratum. The habit and floral structure of this plant are very similar to *A. lawrenceae*, and although the flowers are extremely variable, they are generally creamy-white with more distinct markings. The flowers are approximately 1-1½in wide. Summer flowering.

A. vandarum. The habit of this species is quite different from the others in this group: the stem is slender and of considerable length, from 2 to 3ft, the foliage is cylindrical, and the leaves well spaced out, similar to *Vanda teres*. The large flowers are produced in twos and threes, of about 2in diameter. The sepals and petals are narrow, twisted and wavy. The spur is very pronounced and the whole flower is pure white, very fragrant, produced in early summer.

Angraecum

This is a large and very beautiful group of orchids, nearly all of the species being worthy of a place in any collection. Unfortunately, many of them are extremely rare and hard to come by. The species are distributed throughout the tropical regions of Africa and a few of its neighbouring islands. The plants are extremely varied in appearance, from large, robust specimens with a vine-like habit to small individuals a few inches high. The blooms are usually waxy-white, with a tint of brown or green, and star-shaped, noted for their particularly long spur. The culture for these plants is similar to the warm house Vandas and Aërides, where their requirements are dealt with more fully.

A. distichum. One of the smallest of the Angraecums. The broad, flattened leaves are closely set on the thin stem, barely 9in high; the plant usually grows in a tangled cluster. Although slow-growing the foliage remains for many years. The minute blooms are produced singly from the axils of the leaves, lip uppermost, and are pure white and star-like. The plant is best grown on a raft or piece of tree fern when it may be hung near the glass. Flowering time various; comes from tropical West Africa.

A. eichlerianum. A tall, elegant plant, with a vine-like habit. The stem is flattened, the leaves broad, about 3 or 4in long. The flowers are produced singly, about 3in across, with thin pale-green petals and a large spreading white lip. Best grown on a wall or long wooden raft. Will not flower freely unless given sufficient light (drawing, p 216).

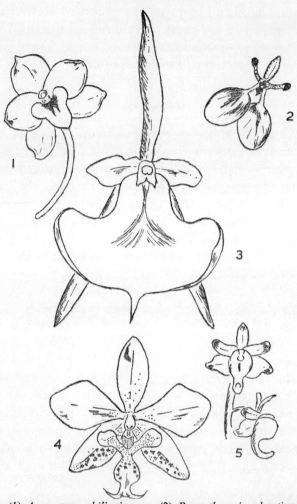

(1) *Angraecum philippinense* (2) *Renanthera imschootiana*
(3) *Angraecum eichlerianum* (4) *Phalaenopsis stuartiana*
(5) *Aërides lawrenceae*

A. philippinense. Plants small with only three to four leaves at
a time, which are thick and heavy-textured. The whole plant
is never more than 3in across. The blooms are carried two to
three on a drooping spike, the rounded sepals and petals of
equal proportions. The lip has a long curved spur. The flowers

are pure white, with an orange stain in the throat; they are large for the size of the plant, and are carried sideways on the spike. A native of the Philippines, there is some doubt whether this is really an Angraecum, particularly as it is found so far away from the rest of this genus. The flowering period is winter (drawing, p 216).

A. sesquipedale. A most remarkable orchid, hailing from Madagascar. The plant is large and robust, with leaves about 1ft or more in length, up to 2in broad. The spike produces three to four fragrant, long-lasting flowers at a time, which are among the most extraordinary to be found in the orchid kingdom. The blooms are usually 7in in diameter, and the spur up to 12in long. The colour is ivory-white, sometimes slightly tinted with light green. Flowers mostly in the winter.

Ascocentrum

Only half a dozen species or so make up this very small genus of plants, often incorrectly placed with the Saccolabiums. Of these only one or two are found in cultivation, and these are pretty. They are widely distributed throughout the Old World. The plants resemble a miniature Vanda and the foliage is often spotted purple.

The culture of these plants is the same as required by the intermediate house Vandas, but considerable light should be given if they are to flower freely. The flowers are small, with sepals and petals of equal proportions and the lip small and pointed.

A. ampullaceum. This pretty species with a dwarf habit hails from the Himalayas. The flowers are produced from the lower halves of the stem, in short upright racemes of up to eighteen blooms. Several spikes at a time may be produced in the late spring. They are of a deep rosy-pink, evenly coloured. This is an easy little orchid to grow.

A. miniatum. A very charming little species coming from Malaya and the Philippines. The stem is a little taller than the previous one, while the flower-spike is longer, holding the small bright orange blooms clear of the foliage. Summer flowering.

Phalaenopsis

A magnificent genus of plants, noted for their most beautiful and extremely long-lasting flowers, which are produced on graceful arching or drooping flower-spikes.

They are to be found over a wide range extending from India to New Guinea. By far the largest concentration of species which are cultivated come from the Philippines and neighbouring islands. The plants always grow in forests where there is plenty of heat and humidity, and are found adhering to the upper branches and trunks of their host trees. They are typical of monopodials, producing a short upright stem, their leaves being produced alternately. The foliage is always thick and broad, but the length of the leaf may vary, as also their colour, which may be a dark green or a silvery grey-green with mottling. In a well-established plant an extensive root system is produced, mostly aerial roots. In some species they are flat, silver in colour and somewhat wrinkled, readily adhering to anything they come into contact with.

The flower-spike is always produced from the axil of the leaf, the racemes being long and branched and bearing many flowers. On a strong plant several spikes may be produced in a year, and a few species may be continuously flowering. Very often, if after a spike has flowered, just the flowered part is cut back, new spikes will appear from the 'eyes'; the plant is therefore continually flowering. This is quite permissible provided it is strong enough and shows no sign of strain. Occasionally new plants will start to grow from the ends of old spikes which have finished flowering. These should be left until they start making their own roots, when they may be removed and potted up separately. This whole group of orchids being difficult to propagate from, such extra plants are welcome. The species come in many different colours and are extremely varied. The most commonly cultivated varieties are the pinks and whites, popularly known as the 'Moth Orchids'.

These are essentially hothouse orchids, where they enjoy an abundance of moisture. The greenhouse should always be shaded, and all direct sunlight, particularly in the summer, should be guarded against, as the foliage is rather tender and will scorch easily. The plants should never be allowed to become dry at all, and during the growing season, when the root system is most active, these plants should be kept wet all the time, with syringing of the foliage and aerial roots, which is also beneficial. Ventilation should always be applied with great care, always avoiding a draught.

Repotting these orchids, with their long aerial roots, need present no problem. They may be accommodated in half-pots, or baskets. They are particularly at home in the latter, the roots soon covering the outside of the basket, interlacing with each other. When the compost has deteriorated, rather than disturb such an abundance of active root, it is best to tuck in fresh compost wherever possible. Only when it is absolutely necessary to repot thoroughly, a little root pruning, especially of the older ones, will do no harm. Several mixtures may be used, but a basic compost of three parts fibre and one part moss will prove a good compost. Where a half-pot is used, this should be half-filled with crocks to allow for ample and swift drainage. Phalaenopsis are most rewarding plants to grow, being of easy culture and very free-flowering, provided they are given sufficient heat.

P. amabilis. A beautiful species with dark green foliage, the leaves being thick and broad. The scapes are freely branched and arching with up to fifteen or twenty flowers on a stem. The large flowers can be up to 4in or more across, and pure white. The lip is white, spotted with red and marked with yellow in the throat. Flowering period various.

P. equestris (P. rosea). This species is of typical habit; the sprays are fairly short, carrying eight to ten small flowers, which are coloured a soft rosy-pink; the lip is spotted. Flowering time summer (plate, p 54).

P. esmeralda (Doritis pulcherrima). A pretty, small-flowered species with stiff, narrow foliage of a grey-green colour, spotted with brown. The flowers are carried on an upright spike, are of a rosy-purple, with the lip of a deeper colour. Flowering time various.

P. leuddemanniana. There are several named varieties of this species, some incorrectly named as separate species, the variation being so great. The typical plant has light green leaves, broad and long, with flower scapes that produce a succession of flowers, one at a time, over a period of many months. The sepals and petals are narrow, of equal proportions, basically white to pale yellow, with irregular bars and spots, varying from rosy-pink to a dull reddish-brown. The lip is small and narrow and often coloured purple. The plant can be continuous-flowering, producing many spikes which will also easily produce new plantlets (drawing, p 226).

P. parishii. A dwarf-growing species which has short, dark green foliage. Under cultivation the plant remains an evergreen, but in its wild state it becomes deciduous during periods of severe drought. The whole plant is seldom more than 5 to 6in across. The flower scape is about the same length as the leaf. The miniature flowers are pure white, while the loosely hinged lip is large in proportion and broad, with two distinct patches of brown. This species is best grown on a slab of tree fern. Spring-flowering; comes from Burma (drawing, p 221).

P. schilleriana. A most handsome plant in its foliage and flowers. It is a large-growing plant, with leaves of 18in or more,

Phalaenopsis parishii

which hang down in a semi-pendent habit. They are beautifully patterned with silvery-green markings often purple on the undersides. The flower spikes can be up to 2 to 3ft long, profusely branched and drooping, carrying many large and showy flowers 2 to 3in across, which vary from a pale pastel-pink to a deeper pink, the lateral sepals lightly spotted on the bottom halves. The lip is curiously shaped. The flowers open fully, with the tips of the petals curling backwards. Flowering time various.

P. stuartiana. The foliage of this elegant species is very similar to that of *P. schilleriana,* although not always so heavily marked. The plants are large and robust, with long branching scapes. The flowers are white, the lower halves of the lateral petals spotted with reddish-brown. The lip is also spotted with reddish-purple. Flowering time various (drawing, p 216).

Renanthera

A small genus of orchids which produce slender stems with a row of leaves on each side. One or two of the species attain great heights in their natural habitat. Their habit and cultivation resembles that of the Vandas. Although widely distributed throughout the Old World, only one or two are seen in collections today.

R. imschootiana. The plant does not grow excessively tall; the long flower spikes are branching and many-flowered. The individual blooms are quite large, the petals and upper sepals are short and narrow, while the two lateral sepals are narrow at the base broadening out until they become very large and rounded. The lip is very small and insignificant. The top half of the bloom is orange-red, the petals blotched and spotted, while the two large sepals are more richly coloured. The flowers are long lasting, the plant blooming freely in the spring. This is a most desirable and popular orchid for the intermediate house (drawing, p 216).

Rhyncostylis

At the present time there are only four species which form this very small genus, the plants of which are of typical monopodial habit, producing short stems. The species are noted mostly for the density of their flower scapes, which are usually produced freely when the plant is grown alongside the intermediate house Vandas. Although only a small genus they are widely distributed throughout the Old World.

R. retusa. This species produces long, pendent, cylindrical racemes up to 12in long, containing many small flowers packed densely on the spike. The individual blooms are white, the segments spotted with pink, while the small lip is magenta-purple. Flowering period spring. This is a showy orchid, easy to grow, and commonly known as the 'Fox Tail'.

Vanda

This large genus with about seventy species stands among the most handsome and popular of all orchids, being grown widely around the world. They grow over a wide area bounded by China in the north, North Australia in the south, and from Ceylon to many of the Pacific islands. Nearly always epiphytic and sometimes lithophytic, Vandas are to be found wherever there is an abundance of moisture and humidity. They are strictly monopodial, producing a single stem and growing continuously from the top. The leaves are formed in two rows down each side of the stem. These leaves divide the Vandas into two groups. In the smaller of the two the leaves are terete and rounded. The majority produce a strap-like leaf with a deep ridge down the middle; the ends are usually blunt giving the appearance of being broken.

The root system is usually extensive and produced from the bottom half of the stem. During the periods of main activity, bright-green tips are followed by a white, papery covering. Many of these roots prefer to remain in the air, rather than enter the compost. They grow to considerable lengths in some plants, and become branched, as in the Phalaenopsis adhering to anything they come into contact with.

The flower-spikes appear from the axils of the leaves, on the upper parts of the plant, but never from the centre. Some may be very long, bearing many flowers; nearly all species are showy and well worth growing, one or two strongly scented. As may be expected from a group of plants with such a wide distribution, their flowers have considerable variations in colour and size. Yellows, greens, and browns are represented, some heavily spotted, also blue, a rare colour in orchids. In most species the petals rotate completely at the base shortly after the flower is open, twisting until the outside is facing inwards.

Among the species, plants may be found to grow in both the cool and intermediate sections. Vandas should never be allowed to become completely dry and watering of them may be carried out frequently, with more attention when the roots are most active. The long aerial roots may be sprayed daily, adding a liquid feed during the summer months. While a number of the species are free-flowering, it will be essential to give most of them an abundance of light if flowers are to be obtained. Many of the shorter-growing varieties will do best in a sunny position suspended from the rafters close to the glass. Fresh air is enjoyed by these plants, and should be given whenever possible, at the same time avoiding any direct draught. The intermediate varieties will do very well when grown alongside the Cattleyas. These plants rest only slightly during the winter, if at all, and this is indicated by the covering up of the growing root-tips. During this period watering should be gradually reduced, but not withheld altogether.

As these plants shed their lower leaves, they become tall and leggy. Provided the plant has made sufficient roots high enough up the stem, it may be cut through to reduce the height of the plant. Where no such roots have been made, these can be encouraged by wrapping the stem in a polythene sleeve packed inside with wet sphagnum moss. Within a few months new roots should have appeared, and the plant may be cut down in the above manner. The remaining stump may sometimes start to grow again. This is a valuable way of propagating these plants. Occasionally, side growths will be produced from an ordinary plant which, when they have their own root system, may be removed to increase stock. Apart from this, Vandas and their allies do not readily propagate.

V. amesiana. Stems short, leaves semi-terete with a groove on the surface. Scapes erect, sometimes branched, bearing ten to fifteen flowers, which are small, white tinted with rose; the small lip is of a darker shade. Usually fragrant; flowers in the early part of the year.

V. coerulea. A high-elevation species from the Himalayas and particularly Burma, suitable for the cool house. The plants can grow to 2 to 3ft tall; the leaves are stiff and held horizontal up to 9in long. The flower-spikes bloom in the autumn, carrying up to a dozen flowers which are highly variable, and may be white with merely a tint of blue, to a clear sky-blue. These good blue varieties are rare. The colour usually appears as a mottling on the sepals and petals. The small lip is usually a much darker colour. The size and colour of the blooms usually improve within a day or two of their opening (drawing, p 226).

V. coerulescens. This plant resembles *V. coerulea* in habit, but the flower-spikes are shorter, and the smaller blooms are of a darker, more purplish-blue, with a rich violet lip, also highly variable. This plant does better at a slightly higher temperature than *V. coerulea,* preferably at the coolest end of the intermediate house.

V. cristata. This is a charming miniature Vanda, forming a short compact plant seldom more than 10in high. During the early summer two to three spikes may be produced, each with one to two blooms. These are a greeny-yellow, while the white lip is marked with deep maroon lines. This is an easy plant to grow and flower in the cool house.

V. sanderiana (Euanthe sanderiana). This species must surely rank supreme among the Vandas. The plant is typical of habit; the rounded flowers, up to 5in across, are flat and strikingly marked. The upper sepal and petals are white with a tinge of

o

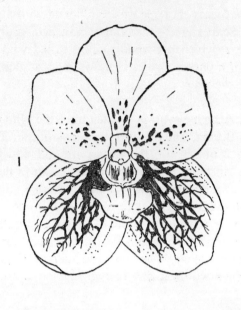

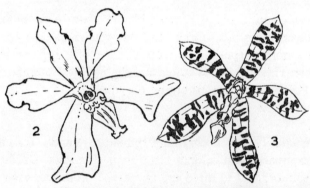

(1) *Vanda sanderiana*   (2) *Vanda coerulea*
(3) *Phalaenopsis leuddemanniana*

pink, and spotted at the base. The two lower sepals are a little
larger and yellow, heavily veined away from the centre with
red. The small curiously shaped lip is coloured an orangey-
yellow. A native of the Philippines, it is best grown in the
hot house (drawing, above).

V. teres. This plant is capable of growing to great heights, but under cultivation seldom exceeds 2 to 3ft. The stem is hard and woody with terete leaves spaced at intervals of several inches. The scapes bear four to five blooms which can be 3 to 4in across. The sepals are white tinged with rose, while the petals are larger and more rounded, of a much deeper colour. The lip is large, much darker, and usually spotted in the throat. To induce this plant to flower it must be given maximum light at all times and rested during the winter, which is contrary to general Vanda culture. The intermediate house will suit.

V. tricolor. A robust plant up to 5ft high, with long strap-like leaves. The scapes are short, up to six-flowered, 3in across. Sepals and petals are pale yellow about the same size, heavily spotted with reddish-brown; the petals twist after the flower has been open for a few days. The lip is purple. This plant, which is quite capable of flowering twice in one year, is a native of Java, and should be grown in the hothouse (plate, p 54).

Hybrids

Most of the hybridising in this sub-tribe has been carried out among the Phalaenopsis and Vandas, with intergeneric breeding bringing in the smaller genera to add form and colour. The classification of the subsequent hybrids is therefore becoming extremely complicated.

Among the Phalaenopsis, which are becoming increasingly popular in the UK are some very fine hybrids which can be traced back to such species as *P. amabilis*, and *P. stuartiana*. These species produced the large, round, dazzling white blooms. From *P. stuartiana* come the coloured lips and spotted sepals. From *P. sanderiana* and *P. schilleriana* have emerged the beautiful pinks, and by intercrossing these with the white hybrids the quality has been raised to the standard of such plants as Zada, which in turn has proved to be a good parent (plate, p 125). These two colours, pink and white, have received the greatest attention from the breeders, and the future of using other species looks good, and rightly so. Although the rounder shape is lacking in the present-day yellows, improvement is being made, slowly.

In the genus Vanda, a great amount of hybridising has been done, but more so in the hotter countries. Because these plants thrive and flower freely in almost full sunlight they are not ideal subjects for our climate. Therefore we must look to the Orient to see the hybridising which has been done with these plants. It was only natural that the blue *Vanda coerulea* should play a predominant part with the primary crosses, and indeed is still doing so. One of the most famous hybrids it produced was V. Rothschildiana, a cross with *V. sanderiana,* itself an important parent. In V. Rothschildiana can be seen the perfect shape of the one, combined with the beautiful blue of the other.

It is possible to interbreed the terete-leaved Vandas with the strap-leaved plants, a famous example being Nellie Morley, which has *V. teres, V. tricolor* and *V. sanderiana* blood in it.

Interbreeding is possible with nearly all the allied genera, and as interest spreads in this field, more surprising crosses are being produced all the time. As the botanists take a second look at many of the species they find it necessary to reclassify many of them, placing them among different genera, and sometimes even creating a new genus to accommodate them. This has caused considerable confusion for the hybrid registrar, as many of the parents recorded are still being registered under their old botanical names.

SUB-TRIBE THUNINAE

Thunia

This is a very small, but attractive genus, the species all coming from Burma. They are terrestrial in habit and produce tall, thin, reed-like stems up to 3ft long with beautiful pale-green foliage of a very soft texture. The leaves are arranged alternately the whole length of the pseudo-bulb. A large drooping head of bloom is produced from the apex in the summer.

In the spring, when the new growth appears, this orchid should be potted up in a rich compost of loam or peat with some dried cow manure added. The plant should be kept dry until the new growth is several inches high, and even then care taken not to get the young leaves wet, or they may quickly damp off. However, once a root system has commenced, and the plant is growing fast, liberal amounts of water and fertiliser may be given, the plant remaining in a moist condition until the autumn. At this time the leaves will turn yellow and be shed from the newly-completed pseudo-bulb, the old one having shrivelled and become exhausted. During the winter the dry stems should be stored in the full light in a cool and dry position until the new growth is seen.

Propagation is easily achieved by removing the old pseudo-bulb when the new one is half-completed, cutting this into sections in between the nodes, and placing these in a propagating frame. These plants may be grown in either the cool or intermediate house, where a fairly light and airy position suits them. The foliage should be kept dry at all times.

T. marshalliana. This easily grown species blooms profusely with large flower heads carrying a succession of up to a dozen short-lived flowers, the racemes lasting for perhaps a month. The delicately textured sepals and petals are white and of equal proportions. The lip is trumpet-shaped, deeply fringed, with an orange or yellow throat. An attractive summer-flowering plant.

SUB-TRIBE TRICHOPILUNAE

Helcia

Only two of this genus exist, which come from the Andes,

and are closely allied to the Trichopilias. Their habit and culture is the same.

(1) *Trichopilia tortilis*   (2) *Zygopetalum intermedium*

H. sanguinolenta. The dull-green pseudo-bulbs are ovate and bear a single leathery leaf. The solitary flowers appear in the the early spring, several spikes at a time. Sepals and petals are of equal size, olive-green heavily marked and barred with brown. The broad, frilly lip is white with a few purple dots (drawing, p 170).

Trichopilia

There are about thirty known species of these showy epiphytic orchids widely distributed throughout the Americas. The pseudo-bulbs are neat and flattened, and carry a solitary leaf. The blooms are produced from the base of the pseudo-bulb. They are usually found growing in the wild at high elevations, and therefore do best in the cool house, or at the coolest end of the intermediate house. After the season's growth has been completed the plants should be slightly rested, keeping the atmosphere around them on the dry side, as the foliage may spot easily.

T. tortilis. A pretty species with pendent spikes. Several may be produced at a time, each bearing a single bloom. These are large and may be up to 6in across, the sepals and petals are of equal size, very narrow, and twisted in their length like cork-screws. Their colour is pale pink, greeny-yellow at the edges. The lip is broad, trumpet-shaped at the base and spreading. This is white, spotted with pale brown. The blooms are fragrant and long-lasting. This plant is mostly obtained from Mexico and Honduras (drawing, p 230).

SUB-TRIBE ZYGOPETALUNAE

Promenae

This genus consists of a small number of epiphytic species which all come from Brazil, and are well worth growing. The plants are closely allied to the Zygopetalums and at one time were all listed under this genus. The plants are dwarf in habit bearing small pseudo-bulbs and several leaves. The attractive flowers, usually solitary, are large for the size of the plant, with sepals and petals of equal size. They grow best in small pans in the intermediate house where they should be kept growing continuously. The compost should consist of moss and fibre or similar materials. When repotting all the old compost should be removed, to avoid any souring of the material. A fairly sunny position close to the glass will suit them, and overhead spraying should be avoided.

P. citrina (*P. xanthina*) This is a very popular species. The short bluey-green foliage is borne on rounded pseudo-bulbs which grow in clusters and readily make two or more growths at a time, making this a very easily propagated plant. The flowers are about 2in across, of a clear citron-yellow; the lip is heavily spotted with red on the sides and base. The long-lasting blooms appear at various times of the year.

P. stapelioides. Habit the same as *P. citrina;* the plants are indistinguishable when not in flower. The flowers are pale yellow, the sepals and petals heavily spotted with reddish-purple. Neither plant is more than 3in high, even when in flower. Flowering period various (drawing, p 170).

Zygopetalum

This is a comparatively small group, the majority of which come from Brazil. They are of terrestrial habit, produce round pseudo-bulbs with plenty of foliage, and the spikes are produced from inside the first or second leaf when the growth is half completed. The long-lasting flowers are carried on tall spikes, often strongly scented. These plants do well when cultivated under similar conditions to the Cymbidiums in the cool house, although a slightly higher temperature during the winter is beneficial. They will grow in a well-drained compost which may have the addition of peat or loam.

Z. intermedium. More commonly but erroneously known as

Z mackayi. This is a very popular orchid with its tall handsome spikes of many flowers, each 3in across. The equal-sized sepals and petals are green, blotched and spotted with brown. The large rounded lip is white heavily streaked with purple. Flowers during autumn and winter; comes from Brazil (drawing, p 230).

General Index

Page numbers in italic indicate illustrations

Plant Index

Page numbers in italic indicate illustrations